Peter Stürzebecher, Sigrid Ulrich

ARCHITECTURE
FOR SPORT
New Concepts and
International Projects for
Sport and Leisure

Peter Stürzebecher, Sigrid Ulrich

ARCHITECTURE
FOR SPORT

New Concepts and International Projects
for Sport and Leisure

With a preface by Frei Otto

⟨W⟩WILEY-ACADEMY

Published in Great Britain in 2002 by Wiley-Academy, a division of John Wiley & Sons Ltd

Copyright © 2002   John Wiley & Sons Ltd, The Atrium, Southern Gate,
                          Chichester, West Sussex PO19 8SQ, England
                          Telephone   (+44) 1243 779777

Authorised translation from the German edition, *Architektur für Sport - Neue Konzepte und Internationale Projekte für Sport und Freizeit*, published by HUSS-MEDIEN GmbH, © HUSS-MEDIEN GmbH, Berlin 2001, Verlag Bauwesen, D-10400 Berlin, Am Friedrichshain 22

Translated by Cybertechnics, Sheffield and revised by Lucy Isenberg

Email (for orders and customer service enquiries): cs-books@wiley.co.uk
Visit our Home Page on www.wileyeurope.com or www.wiley.com

Other Wiley Editorial Offices

John Wiley & Sons Inc., 111 River Street, Hoboken, NJ 07030, USA

Jossey-Bass, 989 Market Street, San Francisco, CA 94103-1741, USA

Wiley-VCH Verlag GmbH, Boschstr. 12, D-69469 Weinheim, Germany

John Wiley & Sons Australia Ltd, 33 Park Road, Milton, Queensland 4064, Australia

John Wiley & Sons (Asia) Pte Ltd, 2 Clementi Loop #02-01, Jin Xing Distripark, Singapore 129809

John Wiley & Sons Canada Ltd, 22 Worcester Road, Etobicoke, Ontario, Canada M9W 1L1

Frontispiece: Sepang International Circuit, Malaysia, 1999. Hermann Tike, Peter Wahl, Ulrich Merres

Cover: San Nicola Sports Stadium, Italy, 1992. Renzo Piano

ISBN 0-470-84698-4

Typeset by Cybertechnics, Sheffield, UK
Printed and bound in Italy
This book is printed on acid-free paper

Udo Dietrich.
Paddling or Rowing
Hamburg, 1999
Poster paint on handmade paper
30 x 35 cm

Frei Otto

Preface

Words are not enough when we talk about architecture; we need pictures to help us understand. A book can help by selecting specific examples, and conveying the feeling for a building, especially if we are dealing with atmospherics, which is the case with sports establishments.

Sport is inspired by the human urge to move. From birth to death we are constantly in motion, even when we are resting. If we do not find sufficient opportunities for motion in our everyday surroundings, such as our houses or our cars, then we pursue it in games and sport.

Like other intelligent animals, we also have an urge to play, to play in motion, even when there are no so-called functions attached. In earlier times, we considered playing games for humans and animals as a subconscious training for survival, in

just the same way as we assign special functions to all modes of behaviour. Nowadays, we see this as a much more complex issue.

We can move anywhere: in a room, in the street, in fields and in forests. Simple sports do not require specialist buildings. Sometimes, for instance, when the climate is unsuitable or there are special requirements, technical aids are needed as well as sport-dedicated environments such as playing fields, stadia, stands, sports halls and swimming pools, to mention just a few.

Sport complexes for schools and clubs are among the most important environments for practising sport in our society. For this reason, these sites must be very carefully planned in terms of volume as well as in terms of aesthetic and technical qualities.

**Competition entry for a sports hall
at the Waldstadion Frankfurt, 1981.
Carlfried Mutschler and Joachim Langner, Frei Otto**

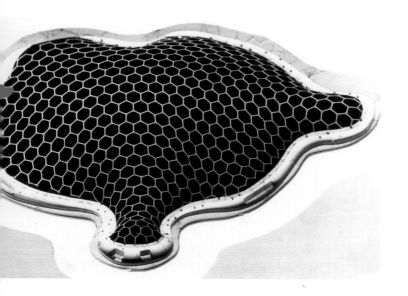

**Design of a multifunctional arena
with retractable roof, interior, 1970.
Frei Otto, Bodo Rasch**

Design of a multifunctional arena with a retractable roof, 1970.
Frei Otto, Bodo Rasch

Popular sport can be played anywhere and makes use of the existing city infrastructure. But it is not simply a matter of adequate facilities. There is a pressing need to create innovative design solutions to make sport more effective and attractive for those in schools, clubs and health centres.

The more sport has evolved from popular games to competitive and tournament level, the more the sports facility has become a theatre for the spectator. Sport is no longer just about physical performance, but also about presentation, the staging of skills.

The biggest theatre structures are therefore the Olympic stadia, which must be able to accommodate a diverse range of functions. They also need to be suitable for other events, as were the ancient theatres. The building of long-lasting

structures for the Olympics is therefore only worthwhile if there is sufficient population density to use them afterwards, otherwise the maintenance costs will be ruinous.

Sports buildings created for worldwide events catering for individual sports pose a particular problem because they require specialised structures. Other uses are therefore severely limited. More often than not, it would be sensible to erect just a temporary structure for these purposes, which can be removed and recycled after a big event.

Temporary structures are more economical in these cases and can even be more architecturally sophisticated. They are very demanding for architects and engineers and provide opportunities for trend-setting innovations; their construction plays a significant role in the field of special projects. Complex, flexible construction will increasingly be needed, such as retractable roofs, which are then only visible when they are actually required.

For larger sports structures in green areas of large towns, the sporting environment is usually immediately identifiable, because the sports area is integrated into the natural environment. For the interior of large halls, an easily adaptable, flexible, environmentally friendly design, suitable for different sports, could be a way forward.

Although public interest is normally associated with larger sports structures, the emphasis for sports architecture in the future should be placed on functional and creative features, especially for smaller sports grounds.

Peter Stürzebecher, Sigrid Ulrich

Architecture for Sport
New ways of integration
Economy and modern living

Where does sport end? Always at the dividing line. Where does money end? Again, always at the dividing line. In the Bank 4you in Krems, they are one and the same: from streetball to the computer in the bank, going to the bank in one's trainers, PC workstations with Internet access and multimedia icons to sitting down – everything is a sports-related architectural attraction. The internal architecture of a sports establishment represents dynamism, youth and success. Business is sport and sport is business. 'We wanted to be different from the usual way of attracting customers, for example by offering gift vouchers and presents,' says Johann Wagensommerer, Marketing Director of the Savings Bank in Krems, a previously unremarkable branch outlet. The success of forward-looking young people both within and outside the bank and of the Viennese architecture group 'the unit' who implemented the Jugendbox project worth 12 million Schilling (almost 1.02 million Euros) proves that he has done just this. Within a year, the number of young customers has shot up by 25%.

'Lower-class' sports and a 78 million dollar salary: two myths which basketball idol Michael Jordan reconciles like no other. 'From rags to riches' is the millennium version of the American Dream. 'Sport', confirms Ommo Grupe, ' is taking on more and more of an events character.' Sportsmanship, according to the doyen of sports education in Germany, is increasingly taking more of a backseat, and it is the media which dominate now '... and hence the interest in advertising, sound bites and merchandising'. At the same time, though, sport is also dynamic and remains unpredictable. Fashionable sports come and go. The Establishment is dethroned time and time again, over which the Rebels themselves rule – even if only for a short time. Streetball (street basketball), climbing and canyoning together with the trappings of consumerism that go with them, is the billion dollar game which is constantly searching for new rules.

Sparkasse (Savings Bank) in Krems,
Jugendbank 4you, 2000.
the unit

The 'new wild workforce' (*Business Week*) in the creative-hungry US computer sector received a voucher for the gym with their pay slip one month. Staff outings promised bungee jumping. And software developer Andrew Peterson, at the invitation of his company, the New York E-business consultancy TIS, brought his spectacular hobby into the office: he is a tightrope walker. 'For most young people today, sport plays a vital role in their long-term development', says media consultant Chris Häberlein from Münich, who has been a specialist in the leisure industry for over twenty years. 'What they want is sport combined with fun and socialising.' There is often a better turnout at parties held after snowboarding or beachball events than there is at the actual competition.

Sport can therefore also be seen as an expression of protest and as an alternative culture. But sport is also business, and mainstream sport is pure. So in 1999, a good half of the 2.25 thousand million Euros set aside for sponsorship in Germany was made available for sport – an increasing trend. By 2002, 1.6 thousand million Euros are expected to result from an annual expenditure of 1.3, according to market researchers from Sponsorcom, a subsidiary of the Grey advertising agency in Düsseldorf. Formula 1 reaps the benefits of sponsorship. The tobacco industry alone is reputed to have spent 255 million Euros on sponsorship. Tennis and boxing are the weakest link, the fun and fashionable sports are the darlings. As for football, it remains a slow-burner.

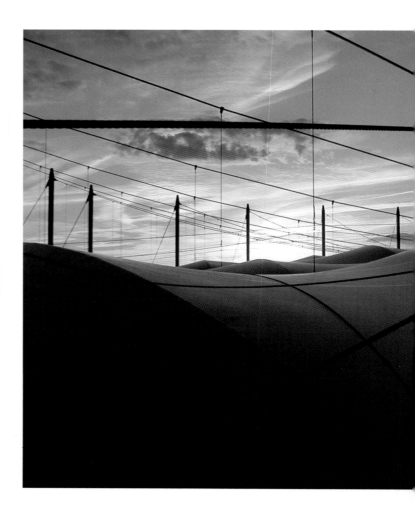

Tm3, the private Münich radio station owned by the Australian entrepreneur Rupert Murdoch and the film distributor Herbert Kloiber, pays an estimated 123 million Euros a year to the European Football Union (UEFA) for the national broadcasting rights of the Champions League. The exclusive right of the media boss Leo Kirch to show first league games for his subscription TV channel *Premiere World* is said to be worth more than 307 million Euros. Shirt advertising alone was bringing in an annual amount of roughly 35.5 million Euros at the end of the 90s. And the British foreign exchange and football speculator Joseph Lewis already made it clear in 1997 just how much an internationally famous club is actually worth: for a 25% share of Glasgow Rangers he paid 61.3 million Euros, which means that the total worth of the Rangers club is therefore almost 255.6 million Euros.

The World Cup due to take place in Germany in 2006 will definitively open the floodgates. If the conditions of the international football club, FIFA, are to be met, investment alone in the sports buildings for ten various games areas will eat up around 2 thousand million Euros, estimates Günter Vornholz from the North German regional bank. The experts, who in the past have been very thorough and accurate, are reluctant to commit themselves to precise figures in their socio-economic analysis.

They waiver between a figure not far short of 255 million Euros and one in excess of 2.4 thousand million. They are talking about creating 130 thousand new jobs.

Almost at the same time the result 'The winner is ... Germany' was announced by FIFA, the national stadium in Hamburg – the future World Cup arena – was completed. The comparatively small sum of 97.1 million Euros for construction costs give the 'low budget arena' an image of profitability. That aside, though, the HSV stadium consumes an annual 6.6 thousand million Euros in interest and capital repayments. The concept of the 'low budget arena' from MOS (first planning phase) and Studio Andreas Heller (second planning phase and implementation) must therefore hold some cash cows in reserve, which are to help ensure that the stadium will also be profitable after 2006. Fifty-one VIP boxes cost 51 000 Euros each season. In addition, it also features a restaurant and a megastore, and a fan museum is being planned. With the option of further rentable areas (7000 square metres), the stadium was in a well-balanced financial position at the start of 2001.

In contrast to the filigree effect of the roof structure made from steel vertical sections, cables and transluscent diaphragms – supported by 40 solid steel pylons – the north German football

temple looks rather demure: the enclosed stands are made from reinforced concrete – nothing fancy added – and only come alive in the spot where the offices of the HSV (on the east side!), the catering and VIP area, the players' facilities, the TV, audio and printed media facilities awake interest from behind a fully enclosed glass façade.

The inside of the stadium is completely different: heated, even though it would be perfectly comfortable without heating, the fans work themselves up into an acoustically impressive frenzy, which generates excitement right up to the extremely steep upper stands. The stands at the side of the pitch, almost within reach, built through the corners and steeply raised, form an enclosed football arena. Hanseatic composure plus a powerful security back-up will not allow any danger to develop.

The enclosed ring carries a price as well. Light and ventilation to an effective regeneration rate and necessary quality are just short of the minimum requirements, and this is not sufficient for a football pitch. Will it be a case of the pitch recuperating in front of the stadium after every game? Even for something like this, the Hamburg business men economise. 'The costs of operational technology', according to Andreas Heller, 'would exceed those of a six-monthly replacement several times over.' So, it is only logical that the HSV stadium – with aspirations to reach Münich standards – will have to get by without an expensive, covered roof.

The HSV Stadium, Hamburg, 2001. MOS/Studio Andreas Heller

That said, however, the city authorities are normally willing to dig into their pockets for the sake of a great sporting achievement: in 1972, the costs for the Olympic Games in Münich were just short of 1 thousand million Euros, the takings were 665 million Euros – at those days' prices. A cycling area and indoor swimming pool in Berlin, both intended for the 2000 Olympic Games, cost 204.5 million Euros. As for the 2000 Summer Games, which took place in Sydney, experts worked out the costs to be more than 2.04 thousand million Euros. However, takings from sponsor funds are in excess of 511.2 million Euros, upwards of 613.5 million from the sale of television rights, and 409 million from ticket sales.

Whenever record holders FC Bayern Münich – for long a world ranked team listed on the stock exchange – celebrate a victory in the Münich Olympic stadium, it seems natural – and perfectly justified – to associate the sporting (and economic) glamour of the southern German capital with the far-sighted investments made for the 1972 Olympic Games.

XX Olympic Summer Games, Münich 1972.
Behnisch and Partner, Frei Otto

Since 1972, the Olympic grounds have acted as a kind of motor for urban development for the surrounding districts, capable of improving the links between the various districts as well as enhancing their status. Residents welcomed the new facilities, green areas, watercourses, footpaths, cycling routes and streets in the Olympia park that were either specially created or enhanced. The concept of Behnisch and Partner meant that the human dimension was respected in spite of the size of the buildings, with the result that the Olympic grounds proved to be a sound investment as a large-scale sports and leisure area.

The basic design of a football stadium is no longer part of the debate. The design of the Olympic park by Behnisch and Partner marked the start of large minimalist buildings as well as the beginning of a light and translucent type of sports architecture. And what about Sydney 2000? After the 'Olympic Circus' left Sydney in Autumn 2000, the city reckoned on 2.8

thousand million Euros of expenditure (generating an income of 1.5 thousand million Euros) for the coming years, and a profit of more than 4.1 thousand million Euros. This on top of a two million increase in the number of tourists and the creation of 150 000 new jobs by 2006. And the calculation seems to be working out: Sydney 2000 became the perfect city not only for Olympic winner Heike Drechsler.

State budgetary constraints mean that standard sponsorship, or funding for sports buildings and swimming pools, apart from major events such as the Olympics, are out of the equation. They can do this. In Germany, the Finance Minister put 122.7 million Euros into sport sponsorship in 1999. In addition, a total of 58.8 million Euros will have been set aside for the 'Eastern Golden Plan' for East Germany and Berlin by 2002. One and a half thousand million Euros were invested in the sports sector by German local authorities in 1991, according to the most recent

XXVII Olympic Summer Games, Sydney 2000
International Athletic Centre, 1993/2000.
Philip Cox, Richardson, Taylor, Peddle, Thorp

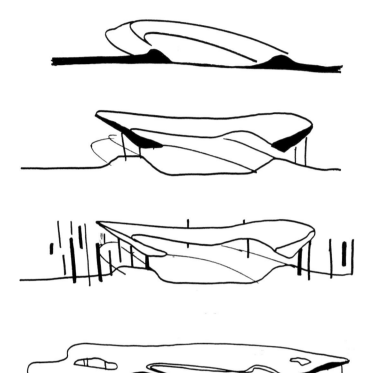

Concept:
A gently sloping artificial rolling landscape into which the lower stands and the playing field are sunk.

The upper grandstand as a sculptural object.

Between the skeleton of the grandstand and the upper stands, there is a forest which acts as a supportive, cohesive filter.

The roof portrayed as a cloud; transluscent diaphragms stretched between horizontal parabolic arches. The construction is not visible.

Chemnitz Stadium, competition entry design (1st prize)
for the track and field athletics European Championship 2002.
Peter Kulka, Ulrich Königs.
Wing assembly: Ove Arup and Partner, Cecil Balmond

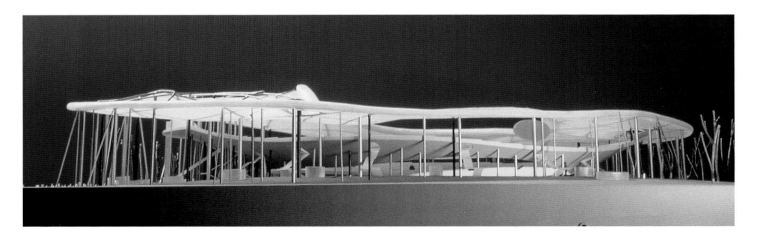

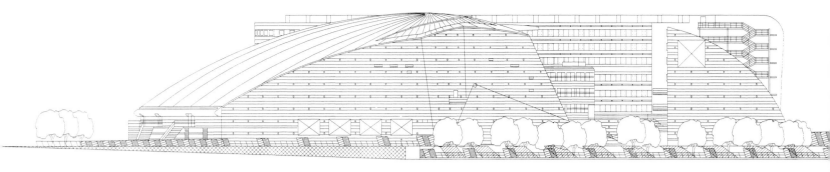

Institut National du Judo, Paris, under construction at present.
Architecture Studio

Central bathing area in Bad Elster, 1999.
Behnisch and Partner

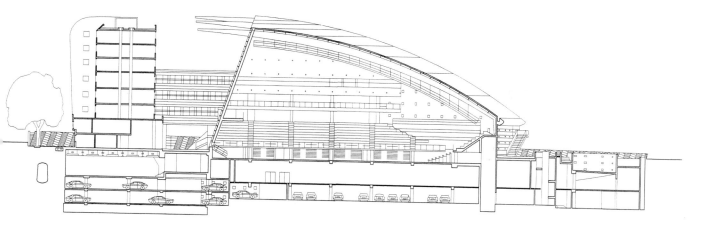

Columbia swimming baths in Berlin, 1997. Peter Stürzebecher

poll by the Federal Office of Statistics, Wiesbaden. Half the 1.2 thousand million Euros structural fund went into swimming baths. Municipal sports centres and school sports buildings shared the 347 million Euros worth of building costs.

And hand in hand with such developments, sport is increasingly becoming a lifestyle statement. For example, only 20% of sports shoes bought serve their intended purpose of physical activity. The impressive 'remaining percentage' are worn in people's leisure time. Since the beginning of the 1980's and continuously for the past 16 years, sales have been increasing, reaching a global figure of 18 thousand million dollars. At the sa-

me time, approximately 46 thousand million dollars were spent on sportswear. Adidas-Salomon plc. also estimates that, whilst this was going on, around 70% of their shirts, shorts and track-suit trousers were no longer being bought for training and matches, but rather as ordinary leisure time wear. It therefore comes as no surprise that from now on, even well-known designer labels have been enticing consumers with sports clothing. Hugo Boss and Escada offer a full range of golf and sports wear. Tommy Hilfiger, The Gap, Donna Karan and Ralph Lauren are likewise fighting for a slice of the cake. By their own token, Nike, Reebok and adidas are converting head offices and their stores into 'lifestyle temples'.

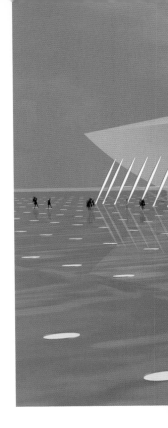

Sport and free time: nowadays, these two terms can barely be separated from each other. Some 27 million women, men and children in Germany – a third of the population – exercise in some 86 000 non-profit-making gymnasiums and sports centres.

Half of the German population regularly takes part in some sort of sports activity. All told, the sports market has an annual turnover estimated at around 61.3 thousand million Euros, and this is an increasing trend.

The German leisure industry supports 5 million jobs and generates an annual turnover of 225 thousand million Euros – more than twice as much than in the building and construction industries. The Institute of German Industry and Commerce (IW) estimates that a family of four easily spends around 15% of their available income on leisure pursuits.

What do people do with their money? Above all, they want to have a memorable experience: be it on a small budget, running in the open cross-country race, rollerblading or playing streetball on the street; or as a conqueror of man-made climbing walls and as a summer skier on an indoor ski slope in Bottrop. 'German national sport', founded by the 'father of PE' Friedrich Ludwig Jahn (1778-1852) has conquered Germany once and for all with its element of fun. 'It's no longer about being faster and going higher and further', according to Christoph Schüler, management consultant of Kompass GmbH in Essen. Today, a fashionable sport needs to offer more than just 'physical education': a great experience as well as fun and action. It also has to be easy to learn, as fewer and fewer people want to stick with the same hobby for the rest of their lives ('sport hoppers'). There has to be the opportunity for exciting competitions; world championships for mogul piste skiing and skateboarding have been in existence for a long time now. And, thanks to television, even 'solitary sports' such as judo, windsurfing or climbing have been able to acquire trendy status.

The sports equipment has to be affordable, such as rollerblades, for example. Media specialist Chris Haberlein still sees no new fun sport that has even remotely achieved the same widespread appeal as rollerblading. But fear not: if Bierhoff, Hassler, Effenberg and co. lose their fashion stamp, then the trusty football will still easily meet all of the 'trendy criteria'. And just like the hula-hoop of the '60s, more amusement crazes – too many to mention – will continue to wing their way over from the USA. At least four dozen fun sports, from 'air-chair' (seated water-skiing with wings), to 'zorbing' (a two-metre synthetic ball used for climbing into and then rolling off) are but a few of the recent imports from the other side of the Atlantic.

If the young sport hoppers need toys, they also need play areas. No longer is their free time confined to weekends. But flexible working hours make it difficult to participate in team sports; organising sport is becoming harder as Saturday and Sunday are generally no longer work-free days. The sports which benefit from this are the ones which are 'independent', self-sufficient and which can be practised alone or in twos: tennis, skiing, surfing or golf. And whoever can and wants to spend up to 77 Euros an hour

Design of a cycling hall, 1999. the unit

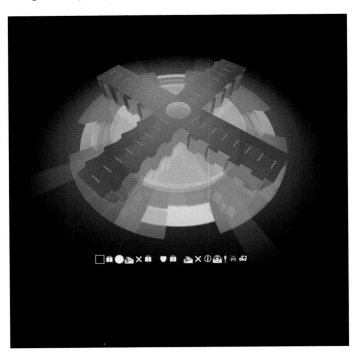

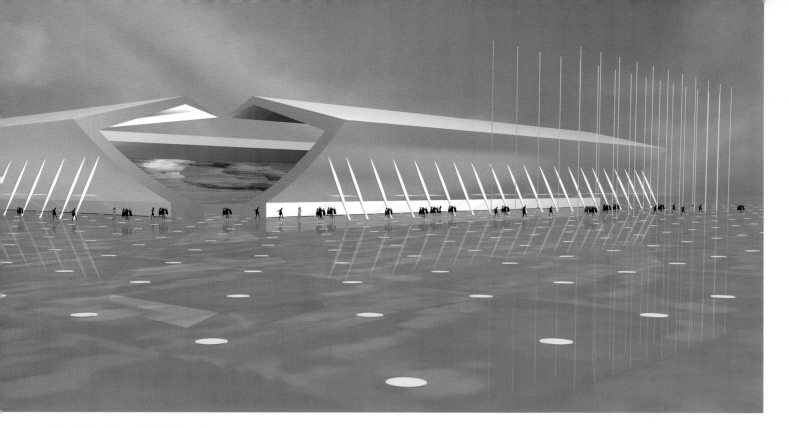

Tivoli Stadium, 1999. the unit

books their own personal trainer, like the Foreign Secretary and late running prodigy, Joschka Fischer.

Fit and healthy physiques are in, muscle-bound bodies are out. Nevertheless, just short of 4 million people are still perspiring in more than 5000 German gyms. What are they doing? These days, the 20-somethings are no longer working out in the gyms – the latest craze for the most disciplined people of this age group is 'drilling' in barrack squares. The 35 to 60 year old gym visitors today are looking for less fun and sociability in sport and instead are doing sport in order to attain and maintain good health and fitness levels for their careers as well as for the second stage of their lives. What started out as a 'Keep fit with sport' campaign in the run-up to the 1972 Münich Olympic Games, has culminated in integrated physiotherapy units with an added gym. Until now '..hospitals and doctors have been for patients', reports the American journal *IDEA Health & Fitness Source*, 'and gyms for healthy people.' The journalist continues by saying that the boundaries of these two domains will soon become blurred, so much in demand is the 'gentle transition from illness to health'.

Even for healthy people, sport is forming an ever larger part of their lives. They no longer have to travel far to practise their favourite exotic sport, or even wait for daylight to appear. The fashionable sportsperson can play basketball in Münich at midnight, go climbing in the Netherlands, play beach volleyball all year round in the 2.1 million Euro leisure centre of tranquil Bordesholm between the North and Baltic Seas, or ski in the Ruhr Valley.

In Germany alone, four indoor ski slopes were under construction at the beginning of the 21st century with costs of between 100 and 153 million Euros. 10.23 Euros for an hour's fun in the cold-storage depot would have to be included, calculates former downhill skier Marc Girardelli, one of the initiators and partners of 'the unit' group of architects from Vienna.

Even the old colossi of sport, the amphitheatres, are no longer safe from contact with an ultra-imaginative audience. In the Arena del Sole in Bologna in January 2000, ghosts were exorcised and the dead brought back to life. In the renovated arena, a scandalous show *De Sade – a sad history* was performed. Dressed up as Roman consuls and in red togas, they celebrated the end of life. De Sade, scantily clad, let his body be adorned with leek stalks by one of his playmates; another grated parmesan cheese on them: the great gorging before the 'sated' slashed their wrists – *Panem et circenses*.

But watch out: the danger of trendsetters no longer wanting such prefabricated experiences is always lurking. Such was the fate of former sports that were once the apple of the public's eye, for example, handball, tennis and skiing. For 'every fashionable sport becomes uncool at that moment in time', according to the findings of Herbert Hartmann, sports scientist at the TU Darmstadt (Darmstadt Institute of Technology), 'when it slides down in "the sports ranks".' When this happens, business trend consultant Christoph Schüler knows that kids will once again gently retire into 'another, private world'.

Thomas Beyer

Mad and Made for Sports
Sport in everyday life

Warming up

The designers of multi-storey car parks will know the exact width and height of the cars that use such car parks. The curve of the bends, the gradient of the ramps, the angle at which various vehicles' doors open, emergency exits and fire prevention measures are all dimensions to take into consideration. The issue of how future users – by users, we mean people here – will be able to move about in such a functional building hardly seems important any more. The results are well known – the outcome really is just a functional building and nothing else.

From the point of view of their users and operators, the design of sports buildings must have different considerations as the function of sports and leisure buildings is inextricably linked with the interests, moods and feelings of the users as well as their impressions. If the design fails to address these issues, we would end up with sports buildings which did not fulfil their intended purpose and that soon became derelict.

For a sports building, there must be certain standards which go hand in hand with its purpose. These requirements are just as varied as their different target consumers in today's world of sport. Be it spectator, popular or 'fun' sport, be it a sport practised in major conurbations or in the countryside, the social status of the user group affects their sporting preferences as well as their preferred environment. Standard sports facilities for the general public are clearly different from those which are intended for commercial purposes or which are market bound.

Sporting trends

In their conventional sense, 'sport' or 'exercise' has not been with us for a long time now. These days, people who 'do sport' come across a wide range of traditional (competitive and achievement) sports which are defined by an internationally established body of rules and regulations, from sports whose rules are agreed by the participants on an *ad hoc* basis each time according to circumstance, right up to the types of exercise which can only be fully determined by the individual. You can experience the whole package if you go on a training course, attend weekend workshops, go on excursions on a regular basis, or take part in weekly sport evenings.

What is gratifying is the supreme ease with which active people today broaden the classical definition of sport by being so enthusiastic in their approach to it. Volleyball has moved from the sports hall to the beach; the mechanics of the game as well

Multi-functional hall made from rhombus lamellae, Berlin, 1985. Design: Peter Stürzebecher, Kenji Tsuchiya, Claus Scheer

Three Court Sports Hall, Berlin, 1990.
Inken and Hinrich Baller.
Use of the rhombus lamellae construction
(Developed by Peter Stürzebecher, Kenji Tsuchiya,
Claus Scheer)

as the rules have consequently been adapted for use in sandy conditions with the result that a completely new game has emerged. Basketball is turning into street basketball – 'indoor' basketball players can still play along though – and has been immediately adapted by rollerbladers. Only the basic concept has remained, that is, to put the ball through the basket. Traditional feet on the ground basketball players are now bound to lose.

What people like has to be allowed in sport. But if you don't sweat, you are not exerting yourself enough, and sport without exertion is – in this sense – not sport. Card games, motor sports or bungee jumping are therefore not sports according to this definition. Armchair spectating of active 'artists' is not a sport either. Football fans summed this up aptly a few years ago, when arguments broke out about the UEFA seating regulations: they held up banners reading 'Sitting is for your arse!'

What does this mean for sports buildings?

Whoever sees sport and exercise as elements of an active lifestyle adopted by many different types of people will be glad of the fact that sports clubs and organisations no longer rule the roost in terms of what is defined as 'sport'. The fun of exercise is now the individual's own responsibility and enjoyed all the more for it.

The juxtaposition of diverse sports is the future to which sports organisers, contractors, clients and planners of sports buildings must adapt. The rate of change regarding the emergence of new sports and trends is on the increase. As a result, purpose-built sports facilities, such as the long-standing DIN (German Industrial Standard) sports hall, cannot be the sports buildings of the future. Instead, we will have to learn to live with a new type of sports architecture which carries a number of risks. On the other hand, it is necessary to develop sports buildings which can flexibly accommodate the widest possible spectrum of activities. Knowledge of the technicalities of sport is no longer enough for the future: the requirements of aesthetics, atmosphere and the communicative ambience of sports architecture have changed dramatically.

These new demands come from newly negotiated working and living conditions, above all from those in big cities. Increasing individualisation, the disintegration of traditional working relationships together with established working hours, and the growing urge to move around in the world of work increasingly rule out 'school-type' sports – training on weekdays and the competition at the weekend. The new approach to life goes in the opposite direction: being able to do what you want when you want; leading one's life without or with as few constraints as possible; liking oneself and being liked by everyone else.

Team sports with their greater time commitment are becoming ever more difficult for people to organise. The trend at the moment is for (solitary) sports which can also be enjoyed in groups. People who stay late at work do not know the meaning of 'after-hours' sport. A morning workout, a jog round the track, or golf mid-morning, some light relaxing exercise in the park during a biorythmic low point in the afternoon, and a long recreational weekend with integrated run-ups, are squeezed into a highly personalised work and life schedule.

The constant role-switching between one's personal and working life also makes some people, who find it hard to live with this, want to achieve 'completeness': not only experience parts of complex (working) processes, but also feel challenged in all their abilities. This search for balance necessary to provide some relief from the demands and burdens of the working world is not new; nevertheless, it is following the same path as the stresses and strains of the world of work.

Why are you running?

Contrary to their genetic programming and inclination, the modern person is idle. Our physical constitution is evolutionarily programmed to protect our livelihood with high levels of physical stress – otherwise, physical decline sets in. So, the archetypal hunt for 'prey' that went on for long hours and days – a workout for the whole body – is an aspect missing from the life of the contemporary 'urban nomad'.

Wading one's way through the aisles at the supermarket in order to 'acquire food' cannot replace this training. The way our lives are organised has elevated the factor of comfort to our purpose in life. And that is not only a moral problem, but also a physiological one.

The consequences: the majority of our fellow citizens are in danger of sinking into obesity and falling ill due to lack of exercise. Nevertheless, more and more people – more or less voluntarily – are discovering the joys of exercise and the sense of well-being experienced in the ensuing relaxation period. They do it for the kick: putting their stamina to the test to see what they can do, and how much more they can end up doing when they practise regularly.

Apart from the individual proof of achievement and demonstrable benefit for maintaining one's health, sport and exercise also offer forms of straightforward communication and social integration – when these are wanted. Sport has evolved from the 'greatest triviality in the world' to the main aspect of our lifestyle: exercise is necessary!

For a sport to be meaningful it requires spatial conditions which enhance meaning. Therefore, a change in basic parameters for construction of sports buildings is on the agenda: up to now, the requirements of the sports trade association's body of rules and regulations have called for certain dimensions, and, as a result, the DIN (German Industrial Standard) sports hall was finally arrived at for certain types of sport. The elimination of distracting influences such as daylight, visible contact with the outside, various coloured backgrounds (so that everyone has the same chance of seeing the ball), and the provision of a precise catalogue of sports equipment, make it quite clear what the constraints are within which such a sports building needs to function.

Creative and innovative (usually commercial) sports contractors do not really concern themselves with this, as they concentrate on injecting a new lease of life into existing buildings by converting them for sport and exercise uses. The available structure, on industrial derelict land, for example, is redesigned so that as much sport and exercise space as possible is created in what would seem atypical, non-sporting surroundings. But it is often precisely this unconventional setting which lends its special charm, and, as a result, gets even people who have had bad experiences with sport moving. No horizontal bar to scare you here; no prospect of bruises and whistles to intimidate you either.

How, then, are we supposed to design modern and sustainable sports buildings, when people only want to see sport and exercise through 'competition-tinted' glasses? Every aspect has to be addressed through open architecture. Daylight breaking, a view of the surrounding area of the sports site, alcoves in the sports hall for chatting and relaxing in, stimulating colours provided by a choice of materials and various shades, windows offering a view, even within the building, the incorporation of saunas or other service areas, the usage of all areas including the roof and walls for playing and climbing on ...

Whilst one group plays volleyball, another can use the sauna. Yet another group can fetch their gear for skating on the court or on another open space nearby in the site; people train on the climbing wall while the follow-up dissection of the last league game bubbles in a corner – and all that goes on without the various activities disturbing each other.

Give me some room to exercise, Sir!

Imagine a building in a town which has any number of sports areas in it. They are not only four-sided but, depending on the position of the construction, are possibly semi-circular or six-sided; they are of varying height, have a simple sports floor without lines, but they always have a good stereo system; occasionally, they have mirrored areas; the lighting can be dimmed and changed to various subtle shifts in colour. Naturally, there are also sports rooms which can be used for regular games, but they can be just as easily observed from the corridor windows as from the neighbouring sports rooms. Wherever it is possible, daylight streams in from the side or from above. The separate sports rooms can not only be joined by the corridors, but also directly by means of a flexible partition system.

Welcome to move (Scenario 1)

The outside and the interior of the building could look like this: you enter our imaginary sports building through an inviting glass door and perhaps you will go past a reception desk in the shape of a renovated yacht situated at a dynamic angle. The entrance area extends to two or more floors and lets the visitor know what goes on inside. You hear quiet background music and already see one or two other people working out.

The entrance area is light and bright, it invites you to stay a while. Information stands with pamphlets on each sport, a board with various sports contacts listed on it, as well as 'wanted' and 'for sale' offers of second-hand sports articles, together with individual glass cabinets, separate the room into areas in which people can sit together, meet up with team members, or have a snack in the café.

Water objects run by muscle power
From: sports architecture and teaching.
Peter Stürzebecher
Interior Architecture: Fachhochschule Rosenheim

The entrance area does not function as a sorting machine for active people quickly coming and going; rather, its function is to slow down the pace. Here, people can get in the right mood or people-watch if they have come too early, or if they do not want to go home straight after exercising.

Perhaps our entrance hall will be a little larger and will have room for an adventure area, the sort that used to be built for children. Who can stay on the narrow beam which rises slightly to a steep platform, from which a shaky bridge then leads directly to the first floor? Or climb down again and then go over a slightly sagging, reinforced former fire hose to the other side of the river – of course, it's teeming with crocodiles here – is it possible to reach it without falling?

The outward-bound explorers move hand over hand along a taut climbing rope situated a metre above this raging river; others look for a hold in the nooses of a rope construction which actually consists of many nooses, and makes reaching the other side less

Streamline toboggan,
Columbia Berlin, 1997.
Design:
Peter Stürzebecher

Muscle-powered water objects.
In accordance with the principle of a
mechanical spider, distances can be
overcome on water. By using tensile
strength techniques and shifting of
weight, velocity and navigation ability
are produced.
From: sports architecture and teaching.
Peter Stürzebecher

strenuous because you can then hold on to a second rope with your hands. Flexible, wide, stable suspended rubber mats are quite an experience thanks to the gentle 'catapult effects' achieved by two people using one, and are the alternative to the see-saw which can be balanced out by skilful weight shifting.

Not only children can learn about their abilites and limits here while the parents indulge in the 'right' sport – the entire grounds are protected with mats and cushions. But one thing is clear: the right of children to have a bump of their own is part and parcel of their basic experience of discovering their boundaries. Courage, not concern for safety, is called for and encouraged.

The courage to move anywhere and everywhere and stimulating fantasies full of adventure develop in young and old minds in the centre of the entrance area. Not cheap, but you get a surprise footbridge: between two revolving corridors, there is a glass bridge situated at a dizzy height of the entrance area. Walking onto it requires overcoming a fear of heights in spite of all the inbuilt structural safety precautions. A real sense of floating is achieved here: you feel a tingling sensation in the stomach walking at such a great height.

The climbing and balancing creation is designed around the concept of a kind of waterfall. Water flows through channels and basins – but only when it is raining outside. Water for domestic use which is collected from the surface of roofs is led over all storeys of the apartment block through channels, slopes, basins, and over water-wheels which drive small sound machines and colour games So, when it rings, knocks, shimmers, and moves the various colours, it is an indication that it is raining outside. And then it is all about waiting on makeshift seats of crates and tree-trunks, or more cosily in hollows and alcoves. These active people also know that water for toilets and the turf are supplied thanks to the collected rain water. The fun of it all only serves to make it even better.

Let your imagination run riot in this entrance area and feel the various materials and textures: warm wood, cool steel banisters, smooth man-made surfaces, and structured floors complement each other. But you really wanted to go to the actual sports area – what you are looking for can be found in workout room 3 on the second floor.

Up and down (Scenario 2)

Are you looking for the lift? It is only available for transporting heavy sports equipment. Only a small, ascending glass cubicle for disabled people can be seen on the wall of the entrance area. Most of them, however, use the long sloping ramp which leads wheelchair users to the first floor and which also serves as a pleasant stroll for pedestrians. There they discover a small flight of stairs which is hardly used by anyone though, as the better alternative next to it lures people into warming-up. A wide treadmill which you will recognise from fitness studios – but used by individual runners only – here is so large that whole groups of people can work out at the same time. Men and women chatter away to each other whilst jogging on the treadmill, always at the same level. Only when someone wants to get off do they climb to the first floor with a final, short spurt, or simply let themselves be carried back to the entrance area level.

Something strikes you about this: stairs should be presented in a much more inviting way not only on sports sites: not banished to the furthermost corners of the building, but rather flaunted, broadly and stylishly right in the middle, with works of art and special lighting surrounding them. A bit like earlier times. Why are all our stairs so dreary and narrow that the people in gyms have to adjust the height of the step when

Muscle-powered water objects.
A minimally constructed, and practical piece of water equipment, similar to the spoked wheel, is developed.
From: sports architecture and teaching.
Peter Stürzebecher

doing step aerobics? Injecting a fun element into stairs is something that belongs to sports buildings, perhaps even with a circuit option over all the floors – ideal for intensive body conditioning. There is even a 'stair race' in the Empire State Building which only top athletes can manage.

There are few rational reasons for passenger lifts and many challenging reasons for using stairs. Do you still remember the warnings you got when you were at school just because you slid down the banisters? Why should that not finally be made possible on a sports site: banisters extending from floor to floor, whose sole purpose is for people to slide down them! There is no nicer, quicker or more fun way of going down.

Or take the chair carriers. On shiny, high-grade steel, you fly – depending on the height – in a protective transparent tube from floor to floor; you feel the air stream by and enjoy the centrifugal force when going round bends. You can keep to the carrier's speed or move on in order to reach the next floor. Then, together with your child whom you hold between your legs, you can slide over to the large carrier.

After your workout, you fancy the fastest option for reaching the ground floor. Inserted through perfectly circular openings in the floor are shiny metal poles which lead to the level below where a soft shock-absorbing floor cushions your fall. After two floors, you feel like a New York fireman when the bell goes. And the race against those who use the slides ends neck and neck every time.

On Top (Scenario 3)

When someone constructs a building for sport, games and exercise, the optimal usage of all areas forms a major part of the planning. For ecological reasons, roof areas are today covered with greenery – but why shouldn't we put even more items on them?

On our imaginary sports site, a large open space for ball games or roller-skating could be made available on the roof of the grounds. Perhaps we can even imagine a 'flying roof construction' that works like an umbrella. So, in winter it is always just as dry in summer, but you can still enjoy exercise in the fresh air. Having a view of the other buildings is an uplifting feeling; and even in the summer, you can go ice-skating on the special surface of the roller-skating area, while someone else rollerblades next to you. But it is not only the ball players who have their open spaces here. Aerobics and fitness groups feel just as at home in the fresh air as do meditative sports fans – all senses are catered for, and physical and mental perception are 'broadened'. The On-Top Area may well turn out to be the most popular sports area on the whole site.

The games and sports area is bordered by a landscaped garden with bushes and flowers set out on small terraces. If our sports roof were especially large, we could picture the sauna garden, a sunbathing area, and small groups of chairs arranged for chatting about the sports to be found all around the sports area or even instead of it. You might even have a restaurant with a summer garden with a view of the roofs of the town – what better way of experiencing the sunset?

One Way up? (Scenario 4)

From stories told at family do's, you know that your grandfather was a real climber. With a hemp-rope, in knee breeches and leather mountaineering boots, he would set off and enjoy the challenges of the mountains from the open countryside. Do you fancy a career 'always on the rock face'?

You can enjoy the same experience in the centre of town. Visit our modern 'Lifestyle Architecture' centre – but you can also do it in other places, as stair areas and entrance halls are ideal for climbing when it is permitted. There are stair areas everywhere in town – but why should we climb them step by step? The undersides provide ideal overhangs for climbing training, while simple bolt-on holds create routes of varying difficulty for children to experts where you can climb lying on your back.

Winding stairs, interrupted by small vantage platforms and running over, through and next to man-made climbing walls, could give access to every storey. The climbing walls are designed so that beginners as well as experts have their own wall where routes of varying difficulty are signposted with coloured holds

Climbing centre
Picos Bello, Nieuwegeijn, 1996.
Jaco D. de Visser

which can be moved at any time. Everywhere on the walls, under the stairs and on the various plateaus, free-climbers in colourful, functional clothing and well protected against a fall, find the appropriate challenge. And the stairs are also optimal access routes to the top rope safety hooks with which the climbers secure themselves when climbing in twos.

Naturally, such a stair area is structurally more complicated and requires more space than a standard solution. But here they are running a unique entertainment programme: the participants have their audience who eagerly follow their actions to see whether difficulties are overcome, or whether the 'fall' into the

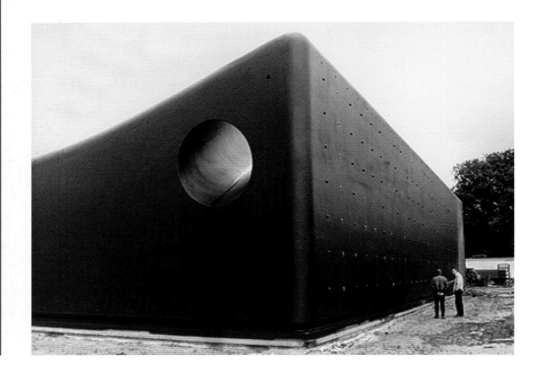

safety rope or onto the mat signifies the end of the climb. This fascinates not only fellow climbers; curious onlookers are also attracted by competitions and warming-up sessions.

Fit for the future (Scenario 5)

The roof, the stairs, the entrance hall, the sports rooms and the classic sports halls could therefore be completely different from the current ones and, yet, completely fulfil the need for exercise. But what is happening in the basement of the building?

Perhaps an underground car park needs to be built here, because, unfortunately, people are still coming to the gym by car instead of by bike (the ideal warm-up!). Shame about the nice space. This needs to be urgently reconsidered, though, as sport and its buildings will also change with the advent of electronic media.

Whoever wants to learn a sport that requires equipment, such as skis, snowboards, surfboards, rollerblades or roller-skates, must be able to learn complicated new ways of moving. How does the new sports equipment actually react to shifts in weight, a varying profile of the open country, strong or light wind; how are they steered and controlled? You know the answer, of course: practise, practise, practise – and a few bruises into the bargain.

I can imagine that this will be considerably different in just a few years' time. Simulation programmes can be quite realistic . There are already video games where, through the medium of the machine, you can easily believe you are racing down the most advanced pistes on skis or snowboards. If the purpose of such virtual games programmes is not to provide 'action' and turnover in

video arcades, but rather to teach new sports, then look no further. These simulations will help you get better at the real sport, but on-site experience of various movements, basic techniques and tricks will still need to be acquired safely and in a controlled environment; you need to be with an instructor, and you will need to practise complicated moves possibly several times. Obviously, people who have had lots of previous experience will get the hang of numerous sports and their real-life applicationmore quickly.

These virtual programmes may well take the same route as classic rock climbing, whose variant, indoor climbing, has long since mutated into a sport all of its own. Virtual programmes used for teaching fundamental skills of motion such as balance, coordination and anticipation skills could develop their own character and gain such an appeal that they become permanently meaningfully and physiologically exciting.

Such simulation and learning phases require a quiet environment in which to concentrate – so, off to the 'underground' with you! Perhaps it will be possible in the future to acquire one's first experiences and knowledge as a yachtsman or woman in the centre of town as the simulation programme imitates docking, casting off, night journeys and navigation decisions to perfection. The whistling of the wind and the cries of the seagulls are provided by loudspeakers; you can even feel the wind blowing through your hair, and smell the sea.

These electronic media could also enhance the entrance hall which we have already described. Why can't we imagine a

WOS 8, Climbing centre and heat exchange station for 11 000 flats, Utrecht, 1998. The polyurethane layer which has been sprayed on protects against the weather and makes climbing and basketball possible.
NL Architects – Pieter Bannenberg, Walter van Dijk, Kamiel Klaasse, Mark Linnemann

mega screen here, where we can project educational films, live broadcasts of sports events, or films from the history of sport. A video library of 'Sports in the Media' is accessible at the touch of a button and shows the attraction of exercise by means of action pictures. Do you think this would disturb anyone? Then simply grab the headphones, and all will be peace and quiet in the room for everyone else.

Even the good old information board could go. You can search for sports partners, sports articles, information on different sports and sporting events, including a ticket service, on a computer screen at any service booth. There are no problems sending e-mails, and the users of our sports building can also chat online about sport and whatever else interests them. You can book your place on the next course, and give feedback to the managers on what you like and dislike in our fantasy sports building.

Have we reached our goal?
In principle, we want to provide open spaces for free movement in an adaptable piece of sports architecture. The introduction of fun, zest, and the vast sum of human abilities to sports architecture has been a source of inspiration to many. Sports enthusiasts have a reputation for never being satisfied; there is always the next goal; more fun to be had, something better, nicer and essentially more perfect to be aimed for.

Benjamin Hossbach

Sports Worlds
Work and Sport –
insider opinions from Nike, Reebok, adidas

Whether in Paris, Tokyo, Dingolfing or Palm Springs – when you look at the streets of each city, you notice an increasing lack of individuality. All over the world, people wear the same clothes and listen to the same music. Even that absolute symbol of individuality, the car, is experiencing a transition to a seemingly optimised standard form for all makes. No longer identity, but rather technical, universal themes such as air drag coefficient, methods of production, and recognition value through uniformity, seem to be deciding factors when finding new forms.

It is an open question whether this trend is an inevitable consequence of globalisation and fusion fever; but a contrary trend has emerged in recent years, one that pushes the emotionally expressive to the fore.

It is the same in architecture, and, to be more precise, in the architecture of large, globally operated firms. For a long time, uniformity has dominated here as well. The architectural tools for most firms are limited to the expression of functionality and/or power. The buildings reach up to the sky and are increasingly shimmering granite palaces – similar to modern kings' castles. At the same time, buildings are becoming ever more similar to each other, their appearances more superficial. The odd example uses other methods of 'speaking', for instance, the BMW skyscraper in Münich, which developed its own identity as a 'four-cylinder' structure. These exceptions in the midst of 'ready-made goods' have been multiplying for quite a few years now.

Conceptual, contextual, expressive architecture which received a positive press, in particular with some large, public building projects, is finding increasing acceptance, even for business architecture. Often the name of a star architect has been bought in in order to improve the company's image, but even this

shows that achitecture as an image-shaping concept has acquired a new status. So, Disney used Michael Graves and Arata Isozaki, and the furniture company, Vitra, developed the image of an almost self-evident synthesis of company profile and avant-garde architecture after building the headquarters extension of Zaha Hadid, Frank Gehry and Tadao Ando.

Image and marketing have always been tools of the trade for large sports companies. Especially where branches which were moulded by global competition and concentration were concerned, reports on their trademarks found in the mass media became part of public consciousness. In this global competition, how well known the trade names were turned out to be a factor signifying the quality of the products.

User-oriented quality helped adidas to achieve monopoly status in the 1950s and '60s. The three stripes stood for quality. Their skilful positioning in all stadia and the expansion of their product range ensured that adidas reigned supreme for a long time.

Not until Nike pushed its way onto the market in the 1980s with a strategy based primarily on conciseness and awareness of the brand did adidas stumble. But even some of the smaller 'old' companies, such as Puma and Fila, had to live with heavy losses during this time because of under-developed infrastructure and marketing weaknesses respectively. In the '90s, adidas took on this challenge and was able to attain record results thanks to new strategies and a general boom in the industry and, as a result, was able to catch up with Nike again.

The architecture of all these companies, however, was just as faceless as that of other branches of industry: administrative

adidas starting line in the world lead, 1985, Martine Fays, 1500 m, Colombes, France

and marketing should come together – a better way would also be after work in the gym, on the basketball court, on the race track, on the golf driving range or in the half pipe. These are 'sports worlds' which should stimulate the interaction and also the identification of the globally active employees with their company and its products. In short: worlds which want to let all the family of workers and their guests experience the most positive aspects of sport – which move sport to the epicentre of the workplace.

The three company giants still have the same one last thing to implement: the development of high-quality, identity-establishing architectural projects in direct analysis of sport. Yet none of the three uses the qualities of the projects as part of their own marketing strategy.

The three company headquarters nevertheless differ massively on common ground: on the one hand in their organisational structure – Nike is building a single tower block, Reebok a comb-like structure, and adidas an ensemble of detached houses. On the other, Nike, Reebok and adidas each combine their own philosophies of sport differently with the programmatic and/or technical conversion into structures.

In line with their philosophy, on the 'Nike World Campus', buildings and open spaces are tightly interwoven with sports facilities. The general standard of the facilities is high, and to enhance status the buildings are named after top athletes who are under contract to Nike, such as John McEnroe and Michael Jordan.

If we turn to the projects of Reebok and adidas, which have up to now only been implemented in small sections, we can analyse their trading philosophy not only on the basis of their organisation, but also in architectural terms.

The close relationship to current product design is pretty obvious. To be sure, it is a result of the respective design directions, but also of the necessary trend impact of the products as well as of the philosophy of employee communication. So, in the administration and research buildings right up to the directors' floors, you meet a cheerful, bold, international mix of far younger people than in other sectors. These young employees who, at the same time, represent the main consumer group, also speak the language of the generation favoured in marketing. Thus, the 'software' of sports equipment companies, the sports shoe, metamorphosed in an almost global sense into the adaption of graphic design on product design. Meanwhile, thermos flasks and even the hitherto cheerless computer design comply with this 'Gel-Air' transparent design; or does the iMac not bear a striking resemblance to any kind of tennis shoe? And how does the structural hardware of Nike, Reebok and adidas react to the language of 'Generation @'?

buildings with washable concrete – or mirror glass façades which bear no relation to the dynamics which embody the firms. The shops – the interface with the consumer – were occasionally constructed using corporate design; however, as a rule only functionality and practicality prevailed here too.

The three biggies of the industry are currently presenting their new headquarters almost simultaneously, and the concept here is considerably more extensive than the hitherto conventional administrative buildings. All three firms agreed on the same programme for office areas and conference rooms, staff canteen and car parks, and perhaps a guest house or a nursery school. Production is located mainly in low-wage countries. The projects are also consistent in wanting their locations to be more or less in the open countryside, and in the immediate vicinity to the site of the company base.

In 1926, Adi Dassler constructed his first racing shoe in Herzogenaurach; Paul Fireman founded Reebok in 1979 in Stoughton, near Canton, Massachusetts; and Phil H. Knight invented the Nike-Swooch in Beaverton, Oregon. What is also happening simultaneously is the concentration in one place of departments which had previously been scattered all over the world. They are also in agreement over the need to play a proactive role in integrating the interests of their staff for whom sport means far more than simply an employer.

Sport stands for freedom and fresh air, for vitality, achievement, creativity, youth and enjoyment of life. The projects of Nike, Reebok and adidas correspond to this ideal by locating their buildings in the open countryside and by combining places of work with high-quality sports facilities. In inspiring and healthy work surroundings, everyone taking part in product development

Nike

The home of Nike is Beaverton, a 50 000 inhabitant suburb of Portland , the largest city of the West Coast state of Oregon. The 'Nike World Campus', 68 hectares in total, was built in two sections structurally and spatially clearly distinguishable: the original campus and the northern extension. Both are designed as L-shaped buildings which house a 'private' room inside and which protect it from the outside in the form of a closed square. The quad is cut in two and is opened at two of its corners by a diagonal axis, faced by Cedar Mill Creek, which runs through the site. In the heart of the two 'L's', the stream becomes a small lake which, together with various pitches, playing fields and games courts, forms the heart and lungs of the campus.

The aim of the buildings is to create a balance between urban density and open rural spaces. This is supposed to support orientation, and aid ambiance and communication. This dualism becomes particularly obvious when the northern extension is added. Here narrow interspaces reminiscent of streets are created more consistently than in the first building and encourage employees to go for a stroll in their lunch break. Not until the quad is closed, though, is the contrast between high-density and green indoor areas really noticeable. Everything else finds its bearings to this 'central park' of the site. Here sport is enjoyed in the fresh air. Surrounding this nucleus is a

**Nike World Campus
Beaverton, Oregon, 1993/2001.
Thompson Vaivoda Associates**

protective group of buildings, and at the rear of these buildings is a circular group of parking spots. Only individual gaps permit a view of the surrounding countryside from the centre.

The first section was constructed from 1988 to 1993 and yet designed as a truly uniform office building. Nike wanted to be able to dispose of it in case an unfavourable economic situation arose in the company. A good 80 000 square metres of total floor area were made available in eleven buildings for approximately 2500 employees. Next to the four-storey office buildings, the Michael Jordan Building with a design and research department was located, as were the three-storey Bo Jackson Sports and Fitness Center, and the Steve Prefortaine Hall with reception area, museum and small auditorium, as well as a restaurant, shop and nursery school for employees.

The first 'L' is mirrored in the northern extension as a second section, completion date – 2001. Predicated on the continuing, economic success of the company, it could be planned on a larger scale, and above all, made-to-measure in accordance with the specific requirements of Nike. A further 100 000 square metres of total floor area will be constructed in nine buildings. In the main offices – administration and research and design respectively – the second section corresponds largely to the first.

By far the largest building of the northern extension is the five-storey Mia Hamm Building, which increases the surface area of the research and design departments (which up to now was 15 000 square metres), by a further 40 000 square metres.

A special feature which enhances the status of the campus is a conference centre in the second section which envisions, among other things, an 800-person auditorium and a banqueting hall for 600 people with its surface area of 13 000 square metres. The building forms the most important interface with the public of the hitherto rather closed campus, and thereby achieves special significance.

Reebok Headquarters
Canton, Massachusetts, 2000.
NBBJ – Scott Wyatt, Steven Mc Connell,
K. Robert Swartz, Jonathan Ward,
Jin Ah Park, Nick Charles

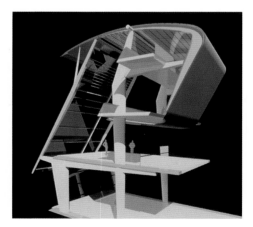

exhibition and conference hall; chance encounters are also fostered. An open-air basketball court and the largest fitness studio in the district at 3000 square metres combine the atmosphere of sweat-inducing sports with the relaxed ambience of the cafeteria and the sidewalk cafés. In addition, the extensive glazing allows constant visual contact with nature and the sports grounds embedded in it, thereby making permanent proximity to sport possible.

More than emblematic for interaction, the 400-metre track runs under the supported building which is up to four storeys high, and encourages communication between test athletes and sales strategists.

The connected structure of the building accommodates 1600 workspaces in a total area of 48 500 square metres of overall floor space. The integral, architectural starting-point of the project that also includes a nursery school as if it were the most natural thing in the world and – astonishing by American standards – comprises extensive constructionally ecological coatings, is accepted with some modifications. The office wings seem almost conservative both in their form and in their classic open-plan organisation next to the expressive and creative 'backbone'. Moreover, these do not seem geared to the development of new ways of working. The guest house, a splendid late 1920s country house that looks like a relic of past times, sets a standard for the whole site which establishes the building in the present and makes the emergence of a pleasant working world possible.

Reebok

The new headquarters of Reebok, completed in spring 2000, are in Canton, a small town with 18 000 inhabitants, 24 kilometres south of the East Coast metropolis of Boston. The 18-hectare site lies at the foot of the Great Blue Hill, in the midst of the wooded and hilly landscape of New England.

While official visitor access to the site with its expanse of water and granite-steel sculpture is still reminiscent of gaining access to many other exclusive industrial areas in the USA, the main building is a refreshing, not orthogonal, expressive surprise.

A spectacularly curved structure, which recalls the form of a stadium curve, shapes the backbone of the complex and interconnects the office bolts that are joined to it like a 'main street'. Many of the communication and development functions, and some sports facilities, have been given a space in the multi-storeyed hall of this main street. General departmental topics are now discussed at a central location in a combined

adidas

Fastidiously designed, the adidas 'World of Sports' in Herzoge-naurach emerges in the context of a more extensive urban developmental dimension. The rapidly rising number of employees, and the company's healthy financial status led adidas–Salomon AG to extend their corporate headquarters in 1997, and bring together hitherto scattered, established departments in one common location. At the same time, as in many places in Germany, a large, former military base lay derelict with the abandoned Herzo Base, just waiting for a new lease of life.

The Herzo Base as a networked system
Competition design entry (1st Prize),
2000.
A/G/P/S Architecture

Herzo Base on the outskirts of Herzogenaurach

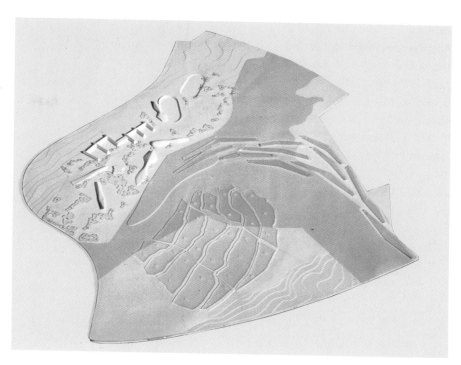

Modulation of the topography in the three areas

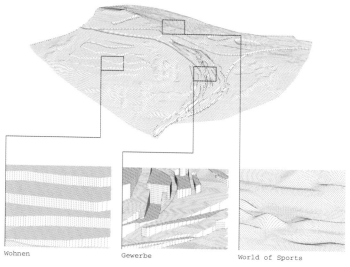

Wohnen   Gewerbe   World of Sports

The 116-hectare Herzo Base is situated on a hilltop directly north of the small town of Herzogenaurach (23 000 inhabitants), approximately 25 kilometres north of Nuremberg, in the centre of densely populated Mid-Franconia. The area is characterised by an old pine forest and large open spaces with wild vegetation.

A general development plan was agreed with the municipal authorities, which envisioned a housing estate for 2300 inhabitants, an industrial park, an international school, a boarding house and large-scale open spaces, all to be built next to the company headquarters of adidas–Salomon AG.

In 'stage 1' in 1997, the only building worth preserving on the Herzo Base, a comb-shaped barracks, 300 metres in length, was gutted and extensively renovated within a year in order to create short-term room for the first 500 workspaces. At the same time, the first ambitious new building on the Herzo Base emerged with the staff restaurant in the middle of the pine grove (Architects: Kauffmann, Theilig and Partner).

The company's inherently competitive philosophy is already embodied in this first, short-term conversion task: a number of architects were invited to submit entries for the building project. The blueprint which was selected in July 1998 was completed in 2000.

'Stage 2' deals with the whole area for whose development adidas–Salomon AG (90%) and the town of Herzogenaurach joined forces. Once again, a competition was announced which achieved the highest standards both in the preliminary round and also in the outcome and implementation.

'The stimulation of creativity, dynamism, efficiency and productivity and, at the same time, the reflection of the corporate identity and brand mission of adidas, the best sports equipment brand in the world' were called for. From all over the world, 226 architecture firms applied to take part in the competition, from which 47 firms were chosen and invited to submit designs (see www.phase1.de). As a group, they represent the widest spectrum of topical, international urban development trends and architectural ideas.

The design of the competiton prize winners (Architects: A/G/P/S Architecture, Zürich/Los Angeles – Marc Angélil, Sarah Graham, Räto Pfenninger, Manuel Scholl) gives each of the three areas, 'World of Sports', 'Dwellings' and 'Industry' their own individual character by using urban developmental and landscape planning methods. Interlinked with each other, they give expression to the hitherto hidden dynamism of the areas through new constructions and positioning, and by sensitive intervention.

All three areas define a common relationship network with a seemingly insignificant interspace which is left to the countryside. This open space in the countryside connects the three areas both ideationally, with permeable, conservatively laid-out open spaces, and also functionally, with streets, public transport and footpaths. All those involved could see for themselves that the architectural result is in accord with the requirements of the town, as well as with those of nature and the profitability of adidas.

The adidas 'World of Sports', with a planned area of 30 hectares, is conceived as a campus of protruding independent structural bodies which are constructed as free-standing elements in the countryside. Together with the two buildings of 'Stage 1', they form a dynamic, open space and landscape structure in which sports buildings and events are linked. The countryside presents itself as subtly modelled in this area, gently curved with varied, natural-looking groups of trees.

An important advantage of this concept is flexibility. The various construction phases could be divided up without any problems, and streets, car parks and paths are adapted to requirements without disturbing the whole concept, as if it were the most natural thing in the world.

View from the public plateau

Staff restaurant, 1997. Kauffmann, Theilig and Partner

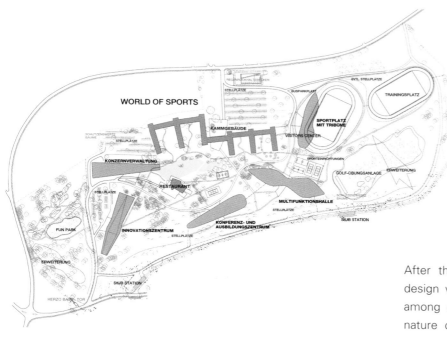

**World of Sports, 2000.
A/G/P/S Architecture,
Babler and Lodde, and
new building by Kauffmann,
Theilig and Partner**

After the competition in July 1999, the full details of the design were presented in a master plan which summarised, among other things, aspects of the dimensions of the site, nature conservation, noise prevention, and coverage of the whole area. The master plan forms the basis for land utilisation planning as well as for urban development contracts.

If the experimental concept can be realised without making considerable cutbacks, and if the particular aspects of dynamism, in the figurative sense of 'sportiness', which the architectural sculptures promise, can be secured in the structures of the 'World of Sports', then a unique ensemble of constructed yet alive sport and communicative workspace could emerge.

Innovation centre in the existing grove,
Competition Design Entry: A/G/P/S Architecture

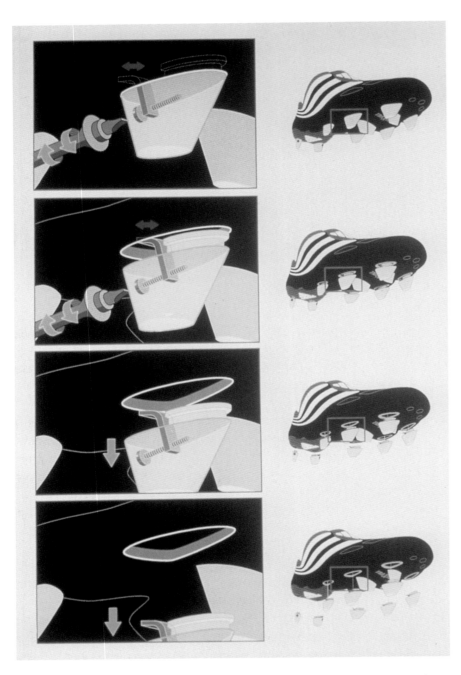

A sophisticated piece of architecture, the 'Sports Shoe Equipment Predator' with competitive design and construction details. It concerns requirements such as comfort and fit, protection and control, stability and grip, ball acceleration and effect. Structural parts of the shoes worn by the winners of the 1998 World Cup – dependent on the conditions of the grounds – were replaced very quickly. The Traxion component parts made from magnesium only weigh a quarter of comparable studs made from aluminium. The borders and shaft of the shoe are adapted to the anatomy of the foot and the performance requirements. With this technology, it is said to be possible to control the trajectory with firm ground contact and direct power transmission from the shoe to the ball, so that every football fan can become a champion ball player.

Judging the competition

1st Prize:
Architeken Städtebau A/G/P/S Architecture, Zürich/Los Angeles, Marc Angélil, Sarah Graham, Räto Pfenninger, Manuel Scholl.

This work carries conviction through its overall concept of openness and concentration. Three cluster-shaped areas, original yet complimentary, rise up within the expansive character of the countryside. The dynamism which has up to now remained hidden within that landscape is transformed into dynamic constructions for sport, industry and dwellings. In this way, an internal logic develops which picks up on what is available and articulates it for specific uses.

The dwellings on polygonal fields are geared to the topography of the site. As a result, the greatest possible variety of plot sizes and qualities is produced; in the case of implementation, these must be precisely specified. The 'World of Sports' illustrates an experimental field made from single sculptural structures. In the light tree grove they can unfold their own world. The team of judges understands the structures of all the buildings which must be defined at later stages of construction. Therefore, the concept of the authors – the spatial combination of work and sport – for example, conference rooms and gym, is welcomed.

Apparently in contrast to it, but nonetheless convincing and logical within the overall context, are the strong tectonics of the long, narrow industrial buildings which run through the grounds from north to south and allow a heterogeneous, gradual development.

The suggestion for the international school as the most northerly stage of construction in this area shows the plausibility of the layout. All three themes together define the competition area in such a way that a higher relationship network is generated out of the amorphous character of a seemingly banal interspace through fluid borders and the new urban developmental positions. It is fascinating to discover that almost all boundary conditions have been tackled and addressed.

The required area allocation can be completely filled within the site of the Herzo Base. The apparent arbitrariness of the settlement forms shows a high degree of realism and gives a feeling of space.

The idea of urban development is applied to the development paths as if it were the most natural thing in the world. This makes an independent development of the three areas possible which both links and helps people find their bearings.

In spite of, or even because of the eye-catching, flexible structures, a high degree of tautness is generated in the true spirit of adidas–Salomon AG: to make a difference.

Heinz W. Krewinkel †

Glass Exteriors
Transparent facings and constructions

Glass Exteriors — lines of development

The development of great, space-encompassing glass exteriors began in 19th-century England with the construction of large greenhouses and palm houses, whose climate protection covers used light and sun irradiation and offered protection from the wind and weather in order to make growing exotic vegetation possible in northern parts of the world.

Joseph Paxton's Crystal Palace which was planned for the Great Exhibition of 1851 in London was the first glass house, in accordance with the principle of the greenhouse, to be used for other purposes. At the Great Exhibition, around 6 million visitors from all over the world were able to experience and admire the spectacular exhibition hall of 'Crystal Palace' in just four months. That inspired the construction of large, filigree glass roofs over shopping arcades, station concourses and inside courtyards, but also of public palm houses, glass-covered gardens used for entertainment, privately called winter gardens.

The architectural development at the beginning of the 20th century was underpinned by the ideas of the New Building practitioners: the first curtain wall of the Tietz department store in Berlin, Leipziger Straße (1900) by Lachmann and Charles Zauber, Bernhard Sehring was a milestone, as were the façade of glass and steel at the Fagus works in Alfeld (1911) by Walter Gropius, the pavilion of the glass industry at the exhibition of the factory association in Cologne (1914) by Bruno Taut, the wing of the glazed Bauhaus workshop in Dessau (1926) by Walter Gropius and the Salvation Army house (1929) in Paris by Le Corbusier, to name just a few.

Crystal Palace, London, 1851. Joseph Paxton and Charles Fox

Curtain façade: Fagus-Werk, shoe factory in Alfeld an der Leine, 1911–1925. Walter Gropius and Adolf Meyer

**Curtain façade as a suspended system:
glass tower block competition, Berlin, Friedrichstraße,
1919. Ludwig Mies van der Rohe**

The design of a completely glass-covered multistorey building at the Friedrichstraße railway station in Berlin by Mies van der Rohe (1920) remained a vision up to the 1950s. From that point onwards, multistorey buildings, first in the USA and then worldwide, were given glass exteriors as curtain walls. During these hundred years, glass technology for construction did not change fundamentally. None of the famous glass buildings was without flaws: insufficient protection against the sun and heat as well as leaks caused problems. Today, these weaknesses would no longer be tolerated.

If glass architecture wants to be innovative, then qualities such as experimentation and precision are called for. The constructed examples from the past are encouraging while their defects led to further development. The development of glass exteriors was supported by a vision whose approach towards reality presupposed the solution of the challenges posed by aspects of material, process, construction and planning.

Glass technology

Apart from its transparency, simple sheet glass cannot fulfil any far-reaching requirements which the market and a growing number of regulations call for. The development of glass technology was not intended for architecture, but rather for the construction of mass-produced vehicles.

Five fundamental technologies have contributed to the way technology is today.

1. The development of laminated safety glass: it began with the patent of Edouard Benedictus in 1909 and since then has mainly been applied as fragment-binding glass for windscreens. Today, laminated safety glass is an important and versatile safety glass used in many different areas of construction. The tough, elastic PVB film which joins the sheets of glass provides residual functionality and fragment bonding in case of breakage

2. The employment of pane safety glass: by having increased bending and tensile strength and the capacity to accomodate considerable variation in temperatures (200 K). Disintegrates into fragments when broken. The first patent was by Saint Gobain in 1929, and was first used in the production of cars and vehicles. Today, this is used for vehicle production: as the exterior shell and in combination with functional glass. Partly pre-stressed glass has been in existence since the early 1980s. It has similar qualities to the former, but, when broken, behaves like float glass. The large fragments which are produced when the glass is broken offer, in conjunction with laminated safety glass, a considerably more favourable residual functionality than pane safety glass which breaks into pieces.

3. The marginal laminate of glass to the production of many-sheeted double-glazed glass: first German patent in 1934, first usage in towing vehicles of the German state railway. Not introduced on to the building site until the 1950s.

4. Development of float glass methods by Sir Alastair Pilkington in 1955: this replaced drawn glass and plate glass. Today, there are around 200 float glass sites worldwide.

Laminated glazing, Siebdruck

Glass transition temperature and low voltage:
Glass Pyramid in the Cour Napoleon des Louvre, 1988.
Ieoh Ming Pei, Peter Rice, Martin Francis, Ian Ritchie,
Michael Marai (RFR)

5. Glass coatings: to mimimise loss from inside buildings through oxide layers and affording protection against the heat and the sun, as well as for the reduction of reflection when transparent. This has been around since about 1974.

Further developments relate to the properties of glass for fire protection and soundproofing, printing on glass with ceramic colours, the manipulation of glass, the use of changeable, intermediate layers, directing daylight and transparent heat insulation. As a result, different types of functional glass for diverse requirements are now available for building, but these technological refinements are still being developed.

Glass constructions

A further important development for architecture incorporating glass concerns the constructive ways in which glass can be worked. Glass façades and glass roof constructions were still bound to material-expensive, solid, primary and secondary structures in the 1970s which limited transparency. The trend towards minimisation of structures began in the '80s – using too little metal in order to increase transparency. Glass transition temperature brackets replaced framework structures in conjunction with low voltage through systems of tension rods or cable constructions. Glass double-cladding and multi-layered glass roofs as climate covers have meanwhile become standard features.

Experience in handling glass grew as a result of this development and made people realise that problem free assembly on the building site was a big issue at the planning stage. The types of glass employed today demand a very precise overall construction, above all when glass is used for a specific purpose and, for example, has to withstand air pressure.

The way glass is used is now set in stone. Innovative glass constructions are only successful when carried out by an expert team right from the planning stage, down through production and logistics, and finally to installation. The disaster of the Hamburg-Halstenbek sports hall whose networked glass dome caved in in 1998 was the result of production carried out by an unqualified firm. In the assembly of the structure which permitted a tolerance of a maximum 1/100 millimetre, cutting and welding apparatus had been used on the building site to improvise and adapt.

However, two classic networked glass domes prove the longevity of such constructions: the glass roof in the form of a spherical cap above the leisure pool 'Aquatoll' in Neckarsulm (architects: Kohlmeier and Bechler, structure: Schlaich, Bergermann and Partner) , and the glass roof above the courtyard of the Hamburg History Museum (architects: v. Gerkan, Marg and Partner, structure: Schlaich, Bergermann and Partner).

Glass covers for sport and leisure

Since the 1980s, a great variety of construction systems and functional glass has been available for the design and construction of glass covers for sports and leisure buildings. These can fulfil

Pre-stressing: standardised glass squash court, since 1970

both structural and functional requirements, not only for established types of building, but also for innovative building tasks.

An example of this is the completely glass-enclosed squash court. The first squash facilities in Germany began in 1970. The fast ball game played against the wall, in which amateur competitions have been held since 1922, and world amateur competitions since 1967, has now spread to more than 40 countries.

The first squash courts in Germany were completely enclosed rooms. In the mid-1970s, Wolfgang Bimmermann constructed a back wall from panes made out of safety glass (ESG). However, this means that spectators can only watch the competitions when the squash court can be observed from a gallery. Only the glass court with its four glass walls makes it possible to follow the game from every angle.

The glass walls in the playing area appear as white surfaces to the players. This effect is achieved through the prestressing process: a fine grid of white ceramic dots is burned on the insides of the ESG surfaces, which also offer a high level of non-glaring, as the white dots provide a diffuse reflection. Small, transparent squares are left blank for cameras through which photos and filming can be taken unobstructed from outside.

The 12-millimetre thick ESG panes are joined to each other with special fittings. Glass stabilisers provide wall stiffening. According to its assembly, the glass court is sturdy and holds up the supports on which the light cover rests. It can be built for competitions in any suitable hall. In 1989, the Austrian Open in Salzburg, and the German individual championships in Regensburg took place in one of these.

In 1994, a school site, whose triple sports hall completed the building grounds to the south, was completed in a confined space in Vienna (architect: Helmut Richter). The 48-metre long sports hall is dug into the ground to a depth between 4 and 7 metres and has a sloping glass cover which rises from south to north by 25%. The glass wall and sloping glass cover constructions were carried out with the patented glass transition temperature bracket system, Litewall. Together with the minimial primary structure, this led to an extremely transparent solution. Prof. Dr. Erich Panzhauser from Vienna Technological University determined the summer heat load under the 1550-square metre glass roof by means of physical tests for the sports hall area.

The result is an insulated glass construction with an outer pane made from 8 millimetre thick greenish tinted sun-protected ESG, a 12-millimetre thick interval window pane plus a 16 millimetre inner pane of laminated safety glass, 30% of whose inside is

Sportshall in Vienna, 1994. Helmut Richter

Covering: central spa area, Bad Elster, 1999. Behnisch and Partner

printed with a white dot matrix. The glass cover system, with a total energy-aperture level of g = 21 % and a k-value of 1.8 W/m²K, has the advantages of demonstrable energy conservation and cost effectiveness.

Prof. Panzhauser comments: 'With the outlined glass cover system which is geared towards dealing with the problem, and combined with a highly reflective silk-coloured screen which lies on the inside, the temperature of the hall could be reduced to such an extent that a pleasant, summer climate can be ensured in the body of the sports hall.'

Apart from the natural ventilation provided by ventilation openings in the eaves and near the roof ridge, there is additional mechanical ventilation. With an air temperature of 18 degrees Celsius and ventilation with unconditioned outside air, the system ensures that on hot summer days, the temperature does not go above 27 degrees Celsius at night. This result was achieved through collaboration between architect, building physicist and product manufacturer.

In Bad Elster, Saxony – one of the oldest German mud spas situated where Bohemia, Bavaria and Saxony meet – the old spa facilities dating from 1910/1927 were renovated and modernised in 1998 and 1999 (architects: Behnisch and Partner). For spa visitors, the site was previously situated towards the outskirts of town, with the spa centre and the theatre. The large, rectangular inner courtyard was used as a production area. Until recently, the mud for medicinal usage was purified here and brown coals stored in the

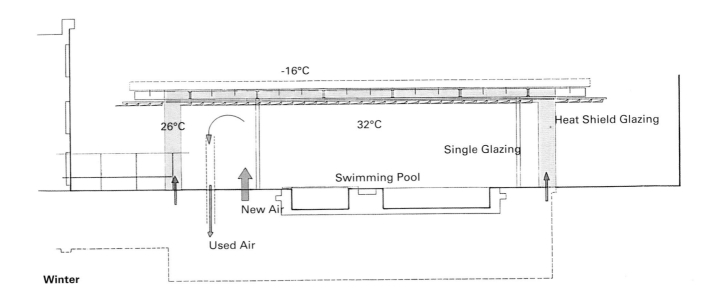

-16°C

26°C

32°C

Heat Shield Glazing

Single Glazing

Swimming Pool

New Air

Used Air

Winter

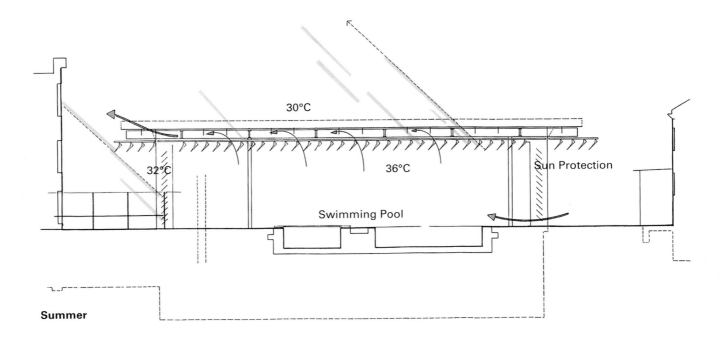

30°C

32°C

36°C

Sun Protection

Swimming Pool

Summer

inner courtyard. The new concept of Behnisch and Partner transformed the inner courtyard into the central swimming area with pools and places to lounge in: an aesthetic transformation from new to old.

In many traditional spa establishments, it was the norm to make the bathing areas attractive for patrons by employing sophisticated architecture. These rooms were the showpiece of the spa. The new swimming pool area in Bad Elster maintains this standard. It is set to become the attraction of the spa rooms, a new focus of attention inside the site: the emptiness and transparency of the swimming area are designed to astound through their architecture.

Central spa area, Bad Elster, 1999. Behnisch and Partner
Scale 1 : 250

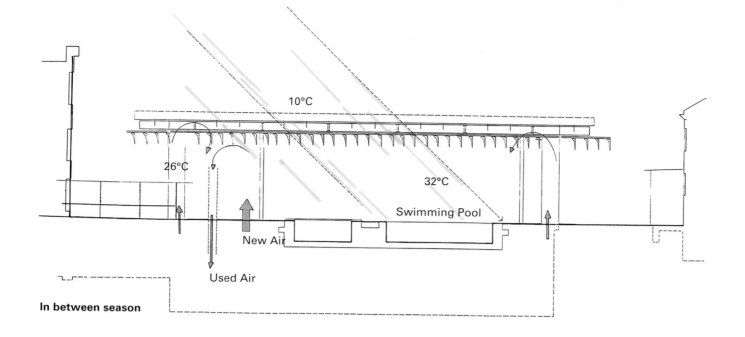

10°C

26°C

32°C

Swimming Pool

New Air

Used Air

In between season

The pool areas of the spa are only covered over with light-transmitting glass surfaces (on/under steel grids with intermittent glass parallel supports), and enclosed by transparent glass walls (hanging pole bar constructions). The roof and walls of the swimming pool area consist of double-shelled glass surfaces with a gap of approximately one metre. The outer glass area is the weather dermis; it consists of a heat shield glazing with high insulation action. The inner glass surfaces are simply glazed.

The double-shelled method of construction has enormous advantages: higher inner surface temperatures of the covered areas, protection against condensation on the façade and continuous protection against the sun. A temperate climate is set between the swimming area and surroundings in the climate buffer.

Preventing the façade from becoming overheated in the summer is achieved by a short-wave, reflective sun protection device set in a gap of the façade. The radiation which is not reflected outwards causes the interspace of the façade to heat up. When there is a danger of overheating, the warm air can be extracted through ventilation flaps in the outer façade. A swimming pool with a glass-covered roof, as well as being aesthetically pleasing, presents an ideal solar collecting point for radiation. It is perfect for heating up both the room and the swimming pools.

In order to solve the problems of heat insulation and summer overheating of the roof surfaces structurally, a second, flexible layer was provided under the outer roof cover. The inner cover was fitted with movable glass lamellae which, in the vertical position, make the outer glass cover accessible for cleaning.

In the winter (outside temperature below 0 degree Celsius) and

at night, the lamellae are closed, so that a climate buffer forms between the glass roof cover and the swimming pool area. This prevents condensation forming on the glass roof cover and reduces heat loss transmission. In between season, the lamellae take up any position. If the roof is clouded over in the summer, the lamellae have to be ventilated from behind. For this reason, ventilation openings in the inner and outer façades are installed in both the south façade and in the north façade. This energy concept was developed by the Transsolar Energietechnik GmbH Company, which examined the feasibility for production and implementation through simulated conditions.

With reduced transparency in the closed state, additional shading is attained by printing the glass lamellae. An outer sun protection device is not necessary here. The requirement is a printing degree of at least 45%, with two printing processes. In order to reflect the largest possible portion of radiation directly outside, the imprint which is pointing outwards is white. In order to obtain greater shade and less of a dazzling effect, the white outer layer is supplemented from the inside by a coloured, transluscent application (Colours: Erich Wiesner).

The new football stadium in Amiens (architects: Philippe Chaix and Jean-Paul Morel and Partner) is a stadium without a track circling the pitch. It is rectangular with four stands, and above them, there are large, domed 'roof walls' made from steel and glass (VSG, 2 x 6 millimetres with a millimetre of PVB-film). The glazing is the outcome of wind-tunnel tests. At the same time, it turned out that the first rows covered by the glass roof are sheltered as a result of the air pressure conditions so created. The orientation of the structure on the site was adjusted to it exactly.

Surface covering: football stadium, Amiens, 1999. Philippe Chaix and Jean-Paul Morel

The lighting of the stadium is installed at a height of 26 metres under the uppermost glass roof edges. The remarkable results are as follows: a simple, clear architecture, an open and, at the same time, sheltered position; an intimate stadium atmosphere through the domed glass walls with transparency and communication directed outwards. The four corners of the glass walls remain open so that entrances are easily found; complicated corner entries are avoided.

Idea, impression and function

For centuries, architecture was moulded by architectural styles. In the course of the 20th century, architecture increasingly pursued the possiblities of new materials such as exposed concrete, steel, aluminium and glass. The latter proved to be the most versatile and aesthetically pleasing material, capable of stimulating the imagination.

A comparison of the history of building, the development of glass technology and glass constructions shows the path to today's

Self-supporting: derived from car construction, sheets of glass are stuck together with punctiform brackets. Every glass wall consists of a firmly glued pane and a removable pane. The free-standing glass walls are held up by an adjustable restraint system. The glass wall system for Aedes, Berlin, is installed securely but also flexibly.

Adhesive technology: modular glass wall system
Aedes Architecture Gallery, Berlin, 1989.
Design: Peter Stürzebecher

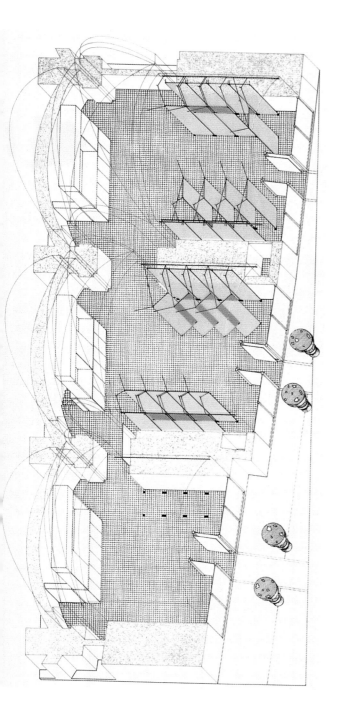

state of technology. The trend towards glass architecture is supported by the general acceptance of the material and its aesthetic attraction. Ideas which initiate new, aesthetic, functional and modular solutions are made possible by technical development and production. Daylight and climate simulations are important planning and decision parameters. Finally, the realisation that glass construction is precision construction is fundamentally important for a piece of successful, innovative glass architecture. Knowledge of the product, particularities of its production, and planning demands must become even more important. If this happens, then glass architecture has a dazzling future.

Niccolò Baldassini

Aerodynamic Expanses
Architecture without perspectives or angles

Harnessing the Wind

In four seconds, he races down the 100-metre long ice track, straightens up on the ramp from a squatting position, ready for take-off, and – whoosh – he glides a distance of 130 metres, a striking, colourful sail. With movement like that, Martin Schmidt would have a good chance of victory. When ski-jumpers soar away, flapping in the icy wind, approximately eight million viewers are glued to their TV sets. The ideal flight attitude results from gravity and acceleration, moments of force and leverage, body height, weight and form, the characteristic 'V'- opening of the jumping bars and canvas area, wind strength and wind targets – plus aerodynamics.

Even when the computed ideal values are confirmed in wind-tunnel experiments, it is nevertheless about getting the 10 centimetre marksmanship on the corner of the ramp, the two- tenths of a second's concentration of the downturn, so that the air flux and aerodynamics will carry the ski-eagle easily and far at the same time.

Sports architecture also zooms in on aerodynamic forms – with an exceptional stroke of luck, it will work if the lightness of the architecture becomes the most impressive exhibit for aerodynamics.

Aerodynamics has been considered an integral part of architecture for several years. Indeed, since the beginning of the 20th century, there have been aerodynamic structures.

While looking for new challenges and constructing his so-called Dymaxion-Skyscraper in 1932, Richard Buckminster Fuller had already become interested in how wind affects a building and thereby influences its form. Starting out with the aim of designing a high-rise building of the type of lightness which is typical of American architecture, he had equipped the building with a transparent and moveable cladding which reacted to wind. In doing so, he solved two problems: the building was protected as if by a shield, whereby heat loss was carefully diminished, and the forces influencing the structure were reduced.

Even if this project had remained a single episode in Buckminster Fuller's creations, the basic aerodynamic concept is clearly discernible. This is confirmed by one of his non-architectural projects, the so-called Dymaxion-Car (1933/37), a vehicle whose form represents the result of the complete integration of aerodynamics, manoeuvrability and function.

Buckminster Fuller's ideas did not receive any attention, though. Perhaps they were simply too far ahead of their time to be understood. For a long time, aerodynamics were in any case not considered as an active design principle from which a new use of forms could be developed.

Ironically enough, it is thanks to their negative consequences, with the dramatic collapse of the Tacoma Bridge (1940), that people became aware of aerodynamics. Produced by rhythmic swirls of air pockets as a result of the constant vibration of the bridge, the bridge's periodic swaying became increasingly greater and this eventually led to its unavoidable collapse.

Yet the rapid development of light architectural structures – increasingly higher skyscrapers, and towers as well as bridges with increasingly larger spans – led at long last to project planners taking into account the effects of wind power just as much as those of gravity.

With that, the increasing significance of aerodynamics required completely new forms of testing. In particular, tests in the wind-tunnel proved to be useful because it is possible both to measure exactly the movement of wind and also examine more

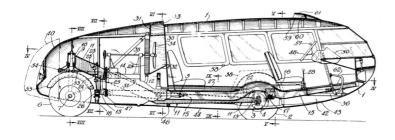

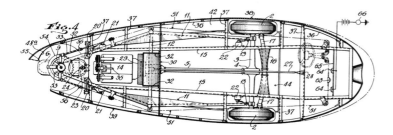

Three-wheeled Dymaxion-Automobile – streamlined car body, design drawings for application for a patent, 1937. Richard Buckminster Fuller

complex, aerodynamic phenomena – such as how structural dynamism and the energy generated by the air flow act in combination.

For example, certain roof structures are tested in the wind-tunnel, as it is difficult to calculate the power of the wind suction in advance. This also applies to high-rise buildings and towers which react sensitively to horizontal wind pressure. If such structures exhibit unusual forms or stand in particular surroundings, only experiments in the wind-tunnel can provide more information about the real forces which affect the structure.

Sports stadia also present an interesting case study. Their large-scale dimensions, their particular form, and the lightness of their roof structures generate buoyancy effects and output in windy conditions which have to be taken into account just as with other factors. Moreover, the roof projection on the open side of the roof above the playing field can produce air pockets, which lash rain and gusts of wind against the rows of seats; in turn, this nullifies the actual protective function of the roof.

Such air pockets can – as with bridges – cause the roof to vibrate strongly, and encourage the emergence of aerodynamic phenomena, which can endanger the whole structure. Here too, the wind-tunnel turns out to be the first and most important testing tool.

The tests in the wind-tunnel are not only supposed to anticipate the effects of the wind on buildings; their goal is also to show and

guarantee environmental effects, that the structures comply with all the basic conditions. Aerodynamically optimised forms reduce surface areas, slim down structures and lower costs.

In all these cases, the aerodynamic calculations and the corresponding tests in the wind-tunnel only represent part of the examination and optimisation, as we usually get feedback only when the project is already at such an advanced stage that very little can be done.

High-tech architects such as Richard Rogers and above all, Norman Foster and Michael Hopkins, are more interested in aerodynamics than others. Their serious interest means that their attention is limited to research into air movements in the interior of buildings, because these are fundamental to comfort and energy consumption. Consequently, they concentrate on convection currents which have turned out to be ideal instruments, in the case of clam-shelled cladding constructions, for steadily drawing off solar radiation heat. Such observations occasionally determine definitively the entire concept of a building, as is the case with the Frankfurt Commerzbank by Norman Foster. Here, the attempt by town planning to attain low energy consumption transformed the building into a type of cooling tower.

The strictly environmentally oriented attempt is called into question when the user can open a window, but only inside of a second cladding which filters the air depending on the time of day or year, and according to a logic controlled by computer sensors.

Furthermore, from a scientific point of view, the convective movements which are caused by solar radiation only represent one aspect of aerodynamics. Other important phenomena of aerodynamics, such as the effects of buoyancy, the connections between form and distribution of pressure, the formation of air pockets and other factors, are completely disregarded.

Finally, the clam-shelled cladding structures are more evocative of solar-powered cars – they consume less energy and hardly pollute the environment, but, for this, they need a complicated energy logistics – that of a sailing boat that only uses natural wind power in order to move noiselessly and, in doing so, brings man much closer to nature.

More comments such as these can be found by Renzo Piano who reacts to the man–nature relationship far more sensitively than high-tech architects. At the Jean-Marie Tjibaou cultural centre in Nouméa, New Caledonia, the structure made from palm leaves is reminiscent of the huts of the original inhabitants on this group of islands belonging to France, and situated to the north-east of Australia. Like a wind chute, they catch the wind and guide it inside. At Kansai Airport near Osaka, however, the

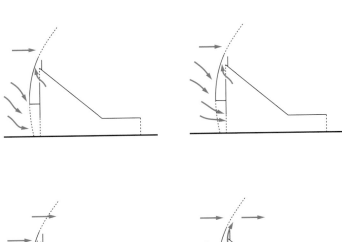

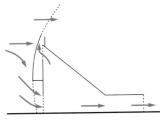 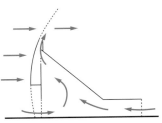

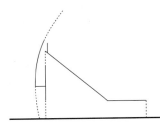 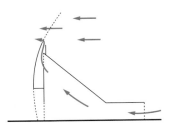

**The Jean-Marie Tjibaou Cultural Centre, Nouméa,
New Caledonia, 1999.
Double façade with passive ventilation system. Ventilation is
controlled by ventilation windows which work in accordance
with the strength of the wind.**

structure and accompanying suspended roof elements form an open channel for the air-conditioned air which, blowing in from the side, is distributed over the entire hall. With this process, lightweight mobiles are set in motion which make the air flow discernible.

Renzo Piano successfully integrated aerodynamics into both projects; with the cultural centre though, aerodynamic considerations are still secondary to a broadly interpreted iconography; whereas structure is of prime importance for the airport.

However, it was not until the beginning of the 1990s that the principle of aerodynamics adopted its own form – from the outset, its laws are as important as other factors, and are actively included in the development process of architecture.

The Glasgow Wing Tower by Richard Horden represents this new approach in an impressive manner. The power of the wind and aerodynamic considerations alone determine the form of the tower. Wind resistance has been reduced as much as possible in order to decrease the dimensions of the building. This facilitates the construction of a very light and permeable structre which is flexible and makes use of the wind, instead of opposing it.

The Wing Tower can be regarded as the manifesto of aerodynamic building. On the one hand, this is because Richard Horden supported his position theoretically in innumerable papers and lectures. On the other hand, it is because of the involvement of Peter Heppel, whose importance in the field of aerodynamic building cannot be stressed enough. As an expert in structural engineering and

**The Jean-Marie Tjibaou Cultural Centre,
1999. Renzo Piano Building Workshop**

aerodynamics, he had originally specialised in the development of the bases of calculation for the sails of yachts competing in the America's Cup. He used his knowledge of sailing in numerous other projects. He conducted experiments to the highest technical standards, thereby continually extending his knowledge of aerodynamics. Moreover, Heppel's aptitude has an extremely positive effect as he does not work with preconceived notions, and is always looking for complete solutions, which integrate harmoniously all the parameters of a project. This is indispensable practice to prove oneself in the toughest competitions – just like in sailing.

In recent years, a greater general interest in aerodynamic built forms has emerged. As an example, let us take the work of Ian Ritchie, the winner of the competition for the extension of the factory halls (Gersthofen, near Augsburg) of the company, Glasbau Seele: he designed the roof of the factory as a sequence of formed mats following and turning round each other, and opening upwards.

Wing Tower and National Science Centre Glasgow, 1993. Richard Horden, Peter Heppel.
The 100-metre high tower turns towards the direction of the wind, the construction is minimised.
The tower weighs 200 tons. This light, dynamically working piece of architecture uses wind power
with constructive intelligence.

 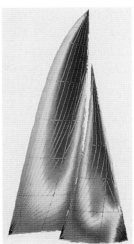 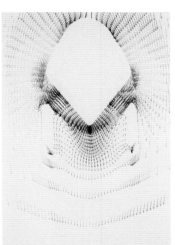 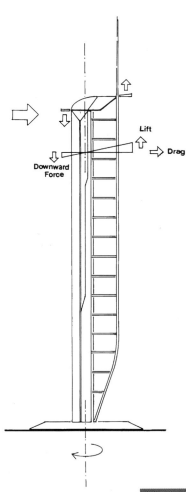

Aerodynamics experiments through computer simulation (fluid dynamics) for the America's Cup yacht and the Wing Tower of British Airospace SEMA. Peter Heppel

Wing Tower, Glasgow, 1993.
Richard Horden

When the wind sweeps over this roof covering, it is diverted, is slowed down and, in the end, no longer exerts any wind suction. The concave, up-ended roof vault – resulting from the roof's own weight – only has to divert the forces produced by gravity, and works like an extremely thin membrane. The raised position of the supports of the roof construction proves to be optimal, both for diverting warm air and for exposing the central areas.

Dietmar Feichtinger and Walter Grasmug used the form of the roof area in their competition entry for a hall at EXPO 2000 in Hanover in order to solve the problem of air-conditioning in the interior. Whereas Renzo Piano chose a continuous, external form for Kansai Airport for this purpose, both Austrian architects decided on a form which is determined by aerodynamics. They stretched together the structure that is subject to prestressing, with a concave, vaulted surface. By doing this, air is distributed inside the hall. Their 'butterfly form' enables warm air to be sucked out at the highest point of the roof; the roof cover is moved, to an extent, between upper and lower air flow. This change in height breaks away from the usual appearance of cable-braced constructions; it nevertheless makes an excellent exposure of the hall possible as it now receives light through the

vertical light bands which are produced in the interplay of the different height levels.

The movement of the wind can also be connected with air currents in the interior of the building, just as in the solar house in Tenerife by Dan Burr, Brian Hemsworth and Mark Richard. The roof here is made from a type of awning which covers and shades the entire dwelling site, and forms an underlying roof dermis which surrounds the actual building.

When the place is shut, the wind sweeps steadily and quietly through the lamellae of the sun protector over the underlying roof dermis. As this has a convex form, the wind is accelerated as on an aeroplane wing and generates negative pressure. The warm air is thus sucked away from the interior of the building over an opening which is situated at the highest point of the roof. In addition, the negative pressure blows the roof dermis up into the air, and thus counteracts the gravitational force of the roof.

If, however, the place is open, the wind airs it thoroughly. In this case, the effect of the wind is lessened by the roof dermis curvature. The wind can spread itself out due to the greater

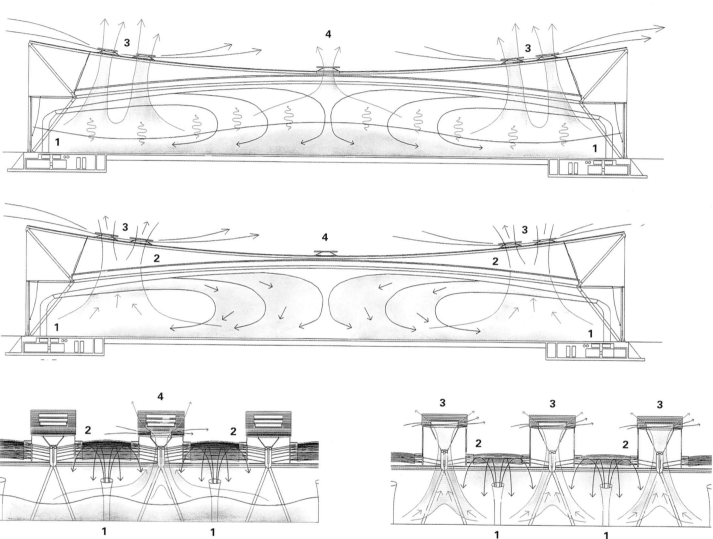

The EXPO 2000 Exhibition Hall, Hanover.
Dietmar Feichtinger and Walter Grasmug

1 **Combined jet of air streaming inwards**
2 **Wooden formed mat as a half-open air channel**
   Curved geometry in accordance with the emission profile of
   the draught – Coanda-effect,
   Suction of fresh air from the park
3 **Ventilation blades for natural ventilation**
   Venturi-effect
4 **Ventilation in the centre of the hall**

volume of space, whereby its speed is decreased. Instead of strong gusts of wind, then, a pleasant breeze blows inside. The wind counteracts the gravitational force of the roof here as well. Even Mario Cucinella devotes a lot of attention to the use of wind power for the climate control of the interior of buildings. His competiton entry for the building of the University of Cyprus stands out thanks to a roof made from giant sun protective lamellae. Depending on the direction of the wind, these capture cool air or take away warm air.

In addition, the air exchange can be regulated by means of flaps which influence the effect of the aerodynamic-formed lamellae by making the exchange of air from inside to outside and vice versa more difficult.

The diverse possibilities which the aerodynamic approach offers have led to a scientific research project which is financed by the European Union. In this project, Cucinella uses the air flow by capturing the air over vertical 'wind-catchers', which is then sprayed into water, and finally vaporised. The change of state from liquid into gas extracts heat from the air. The air cooled down in this way descends and distributes itself – only as a result of the difference in weight and pressure – throughout the entire building.

Basically, this means that, on an urban scale, the form of all building complexes influences all environmental conditions, and therefore also those of large, open spaces. The design by Richard Horden for the building of the Scottish National Science Centre in Glasgow comes from such an approach – an exhibition site with three pavilions, in which the Wing Tower is also to be integrated.

Each of these pavilions consists of two basic elements: the actual building structure and the virtual roof lying over it; virtual because it circumscribes a space without actually locking up a real volume of space. This is because it consists merely of a sturdy net made from open, square holes.

The wind sweeps through these holes and slows down because numerous small air pockets form at the edges of the net. As through a row of trees or a hedgerow, the virtual dome of wind pressure is sheltered. Between the roof dermis of the exhibition building and the virtual dome, an interspace forms which is perfectly suitable as an exhibition area since it is open but nevertheless protected.

In connection with large, urban projects, the Zed (Zero Emission Development project of Future Systems) (1995) should also be mentioned. Here, the architects from the London group, Future Systems, were bold enough to transform a residential building into a type of wind machine set to town scale. Through the winding, outer form of the building, the air flow is accelerated and directed through a central opening into the interior, where wind energy is generated in a pipe equipped with a turbine.

In spite of all these new observations, aerodynamics has, up to now, not really found its way into the planning of large sports stadia, although it would be of fundamental importance here.

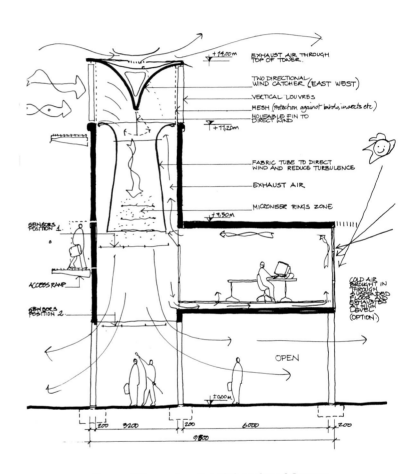

Competition entry, the University of Cyprus.
Mario Cucinella

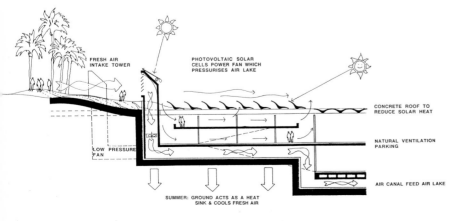

EU research project, Joule, 1995.
Passive cooling system through vaporising.
Mario Cucinella

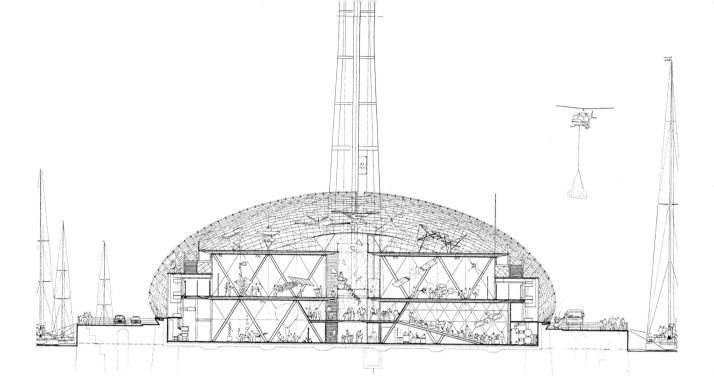

National Science Centre Glasgow.
Richard Horden, Peter Heppel.
Light architecture dome, the form of which is similar to that of a water-drop in order to reduce the effects of the wind with 'droplet-dome' geometry: a total weight of 40 tons is calculated for the 52 metre dome.

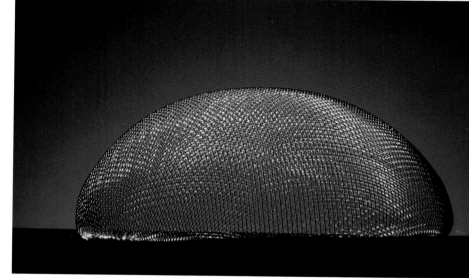

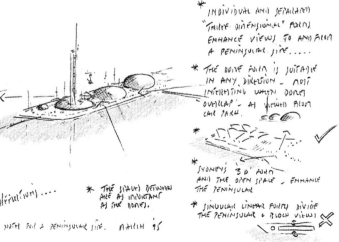

Overall concept, National Science Centre Glasgow

But in this field, the great architectural gesture still dominates over new technological discoveries and new ideas. Moreover, in the current architectural debate, no one is allowed to disregard the fact that architectural innovations are mostly tested far from public planning in small and medium-sized projects.

An example of aerodynamics consideration is the Sydney football stadium which was built in 1988 by Philip Cox, Richardson, Taylor and Partner. With great attention to detail, they tried to optimise the effect of air currents here. For this, the architectural requirements already stipulated had, of course, still to be taken into account.

Football stadium, Amiens, 1999.
Philippe Chaix and Jean-Paul Morel

A vent was cut at the edge of the roof covering. When the air brushes against the roof, it flows through the vent. In doing so, the differences in pressure decrease. In this way, the formation of larger air pockets can be prevented, which could otherwise easily damage such large structures. Moreover, the central part of the roof covering, which is made from perforated aluminium bands, is constructed in such a way that the pressure from inside and outside affects two surfaces. Thus, the effects offset each other, and the wind suction on the roof decreases altogether.

Technological progress is not held back even in stadia: even here, there are already some signs of a fundamental change in methods of construction. With his sports stadium in Bari, Renzo Piano proved that a roof over a sports site can be more than the usual weather protector. Specifically tailored to the special conditions of the hot climate in southern Italy, he constructed a roof that acts like a parasol in affording protection against the sun, and at the same time is extremely light and wind-permeable.

The new football stadium in Amiens, designed by Philippe Chaix and Jean-Paul Morel, is similarly formed. In order to satisfy the environmental constraints of the site, the architects used a different material for the same, outer form of the roof. In this case, the round surface made from glass serves as a wind and rain shield. Warming rays of sunshine can, however, penetrate the transparent material and thereby pleasantly adjust the temperature for the spectators.

San Nicola Sports Stadium in Bari, 1990.
Renzo Piano Building Workshop

Football stadium, Sydney, Australia 2000.
Philip Cox, Richardson, Taylor and Partner

Both stadia have a similar form, both react sensitively to the wind. Both were therefore tested in the wind-tunnel. They differ from prevailing concepts of sports stadia above all because of the novel function of the roof.

While the roof of the stadium in Bari only protects against the sun, but lets rain in, the roof in Amiens keeps out the rain and lets light and warmth through. Neither corresponds to the traditional protective function of the roof.

If we were to build a roof that could react to airflow, it would still only be a small step towards a completely aerodynamic concept in which the wind itself determined the form.

Today, aerodynamic construction has grown out of its embryonic developmental stage. This also shows that the architect in particular is no longer only starting out from the principles of aviation, from which aerodynamics as a discipline is derived, but rather that aerodynamics is finding its own identity.

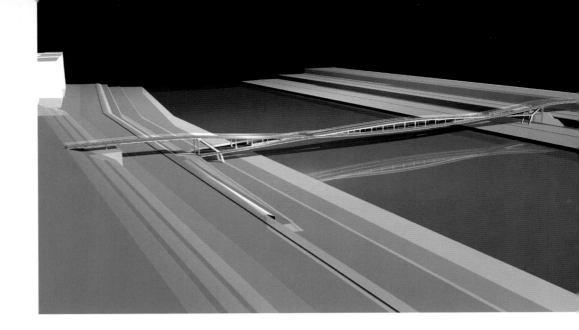

Bridge, grandstand, footbridge
over the Seine,
Bercy-Tolbiac, Paris,
currently under construction.
Dietmar Feichtinger and
Walter Grasmug

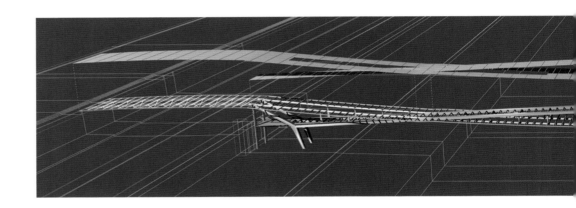

Aerodynamics is already used as a tool by high-tech companies in order to build environmentally friendly buildings with bio-sensitive air-conditioning and low energy consumption. Now, we are finally at such an advanced stage that we do take aerodynamics – giving it the same importance as other factors – into consideration at the planning stage in terms of a balanced logic, both with regard to the architectural structure and to the prevailing environment. The aim here must be to establish eco-friendliness as a quality feature of modern construction.

As such, the aerodynamic approach offers many new solutions which can improve architecture. It is now possible to design constructions which correspond to individual needs and to the environment more closely, as they are increasingly based on an all-embracing, ecological worldview.

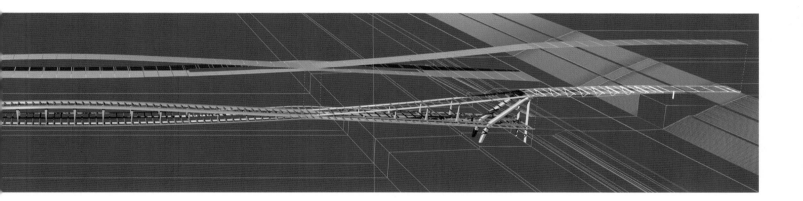

Grandstand over the Seine, Paris:
Two curves produce the geometry of the bridge. The curves are simultaneously a supporting construction and a
guide. They form a broadly spanning pressured curve and tie rod. The interaction of the two elements makes the
open span of 190 metres possible. In the central area of the bridge, the overlapping of bend and tie rod generates
an aerodynamically optimised volume (Consultancy: Niccolò Baldassini, RFR) in the form of a lens – as a grandstand
for sports events on the water.

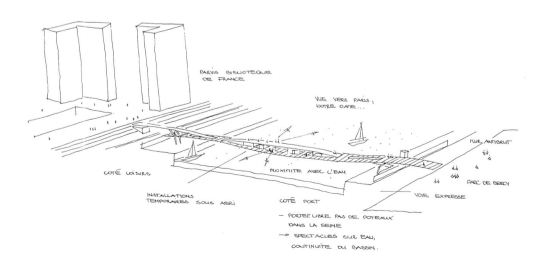

Swimming pool by the Atlantic Ocean,
Piscina en Leça da Palmeira,
Portugal, 1965.
Alvaro Siza

Peter Stürzebecher, Sigrid Ulrich

25 International Projects
Stadia Stands Sports Halls Swimming Pools Museums/Institutes

Philip Cox, Richardson, Taylor, Peddle, Thorp

International Athletic Centre
The Summer Olympic Games, Sydney 2000
Australia – Sydney – Homebush Bay

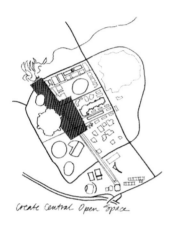

Create Central Open Space

'The best Olympic Games ever' and the 'the nicest and friendliest' enthused a crowd of a thousand million people in Sydney 2000. Jörn Utzon's Opera House, softly steeped in changing colour schemes, meets the sporting frenzy. Sydney's Homebush Bay has a developmental objective that is more extensive than similar Olympic sites around the world. A compact Olympic Games area was designed in order to house most of the Olympic facilities in one cohesive sports site. Above all, though, the masterplan secures the sustainability of the area after the games. This includes imposing new parks, bigger than New York's Central Park, residential areas which are situated close to the countryside, new retail and living spaces and further facilities for the Olympic sports enterprise.

Since the 19th century, these grounds have been used respectively as a racecourse, a brickworks, a weapons depot for the navy and as an abattoir, polluted by industry and household waste. The hosting of Olympic Games provided the opportunity to make the area accessible to the public and to create a new, diverse and useful area for Sydney as well as for the whole of Australia.

Engage Major Buildings

A town and infrastructure of integrated train networks, buses and ferries made access easier. A ferry connected the northern end of the site with the Olympic Boulevard, the main arterial road. From here, 500 000 visitors daily would walk along the boulevard, one and a half kilometres long, with which the most important sites for the 2000 Games interconnected.

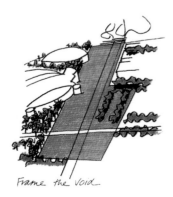

Frame the Void

**Three structures:
the red structure forms a paved
centre, the green joins the countryside
with the surrounding parks, the blue
structure indicates water.**

Emphasize High Point

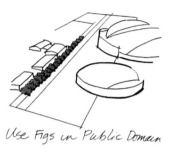

Use Figs in Public Domain

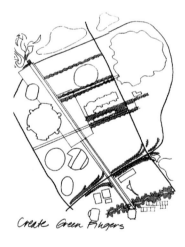

Create Green Fingers

Water at High and Low Points

Masterplan of the Olympic Games site in Homebush. George Hargreaves. Scale 1 : 10 000

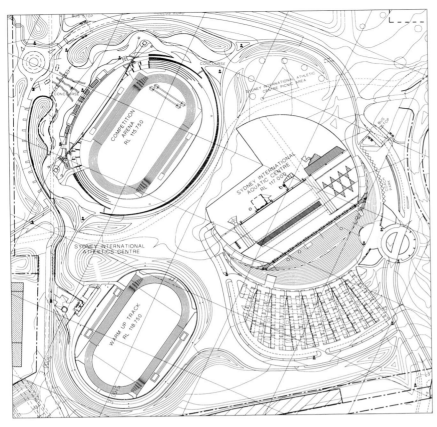

Sydney International Athletic Centre, 1993/2000.
Philip Cox, Richardson, Taylor, Peddle, Thorp Architects
Scale 1 : 5 000

Dominated by the Millennium Parklands, a row of smaller buildings and sites is situated at the northern end of the area, for instance, the Olympic village, Newington (a living area for 4 500 inhabitants, but housing 15 300 people during the Games) and the romantic Sydney International Archery Park (Stutchbury and Pape). This is a 100 x 10 metre large pavilion, lined with recycled hardwood, and a roof with open, translucent ceilings allowing for natural light and ventilation.

Whoever steps out onto the Olympic Boulevard notices the Sydney Super Dome first (Cox, Richardson, Devine, Defllon, Yaeger). This completely closed arena with 20 000 seats is the largest, totally enclosed hall in the southern hemisphere. Steel pinnacles stand in solitary splendour on the dome and create an outer maintenance structure which makes extensive installations on the inside superfluous, and provide an unobstructed view of Olympic gymnastics and basketball events.

The Sydney Showgrounds opposite are spread out with the Exhibition Halls, above them is the 'Australian Pantheon' for 10 000 spectators (Ancher, Mortlock and Woolley) and the Animal Pavilions extending over 30 hectares. There is also a place for the baseball showring (Philip Cox, Richardson, Conybeare, Morrison, Peddle, Thorp Architects) and several satellite pavilions.

If you wander further along the boulevard, the 'Australia stadium' is the next to come into view with its characteristic dome structure. Designed by Bligh Lobb Sports Architects in co-operation with Bligh, Voller, Nield, the stadium accommodates 123 000 spectators. It is the largest Olympic stadium since 1972 and was the scene of the most important sporting events of the Games, the opening and closing ceremonies, as well as the football final.

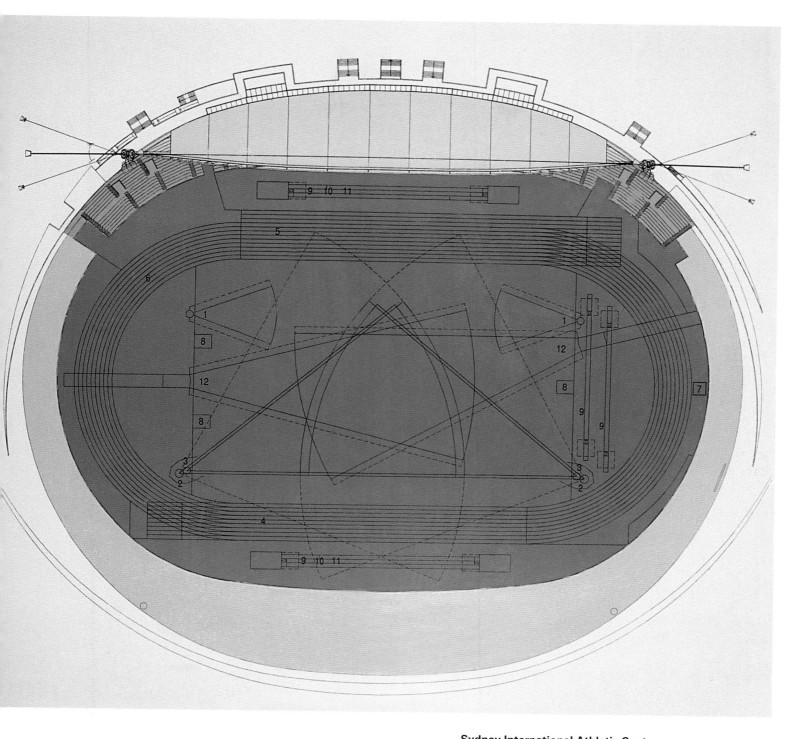

Sydney International Athletic Centre,
1993/2000. Scale 1 : 1000
Seven years before the start of construction for the
Olympic Games, the International Athletic Centre
was used in various ways as a stadium for track
and field athletics, competitions and
warming-up. The suspended roof of the west
stands is in the style of 'light architecture' as a
cable-braced construction, suspended on two
masts, dispersed in curved columns and pull ropes,
and, consequently, is extremely minimal.

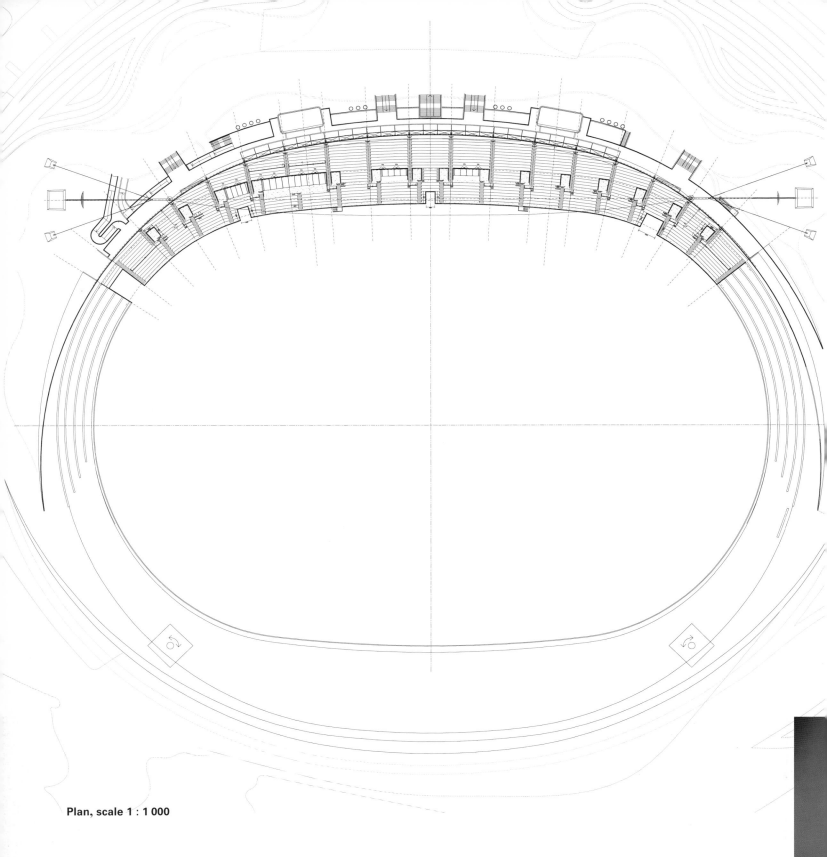

Plan, scale 1 : 1 000

If you take the Olympia-Express, you arrive at the centre of the site, and alight near the Olympic Park railway station – an 'architectural fanfare' created from a single, dramatic gesture. Effective through the neatly spread-out fanlights, penetrating light creates a surprisingly soft, filigree structure out of the roof framework. The train station could take up to 50 000 passengers or 30 trains every hour. The Homebush Bay Novotel Ibis hotel is the highest building in the centre of the Olympic Games site and therefore serves as an important point of reference. Nearby are the Sydney International Aquatic Centre and the Sydney International Athletics Centre (both by Philip Cox, Richardson, Taylor, Peddle, Thorp Architects).

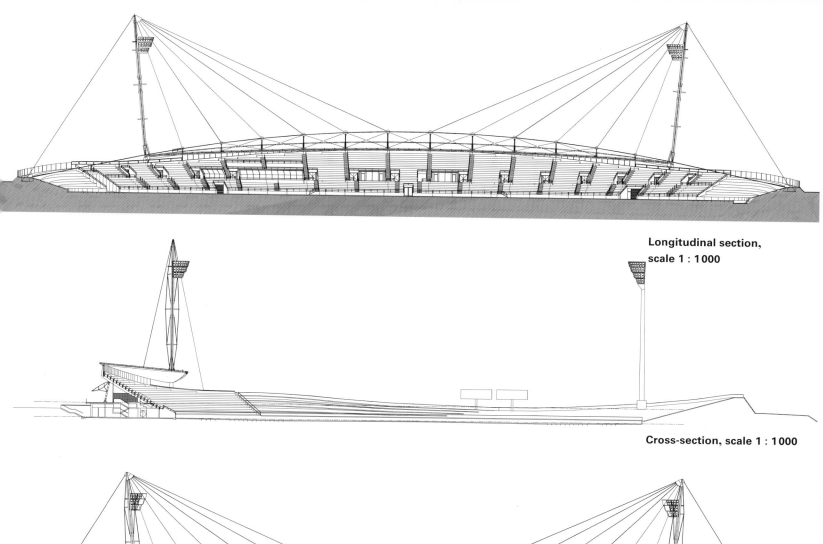

Longitudinal section,
scale 1 : 1000

Cross-section, scale 1 : 1000

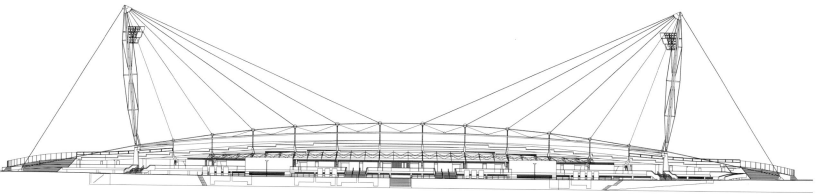

View of the western side,
scale 1 : 1000

The swimming and diving facilities of the Sydney International Aquatic Centre were designed in such a way as to be of maximum use to the public before and after the Games. Consequently, there are three larger diving, competition and trainings pools, and a large leisure pool with water slides, waterfalls and whirlpool baths, all fitted into abstract mosaics of marine animals. The stream of light from the steel roof was moulded so that it enhances kinetic effects. At night, a steel structure forms a dome out of the landscape. The dome is constructed so that the wall underneath it can be removed and, during the Games, additional seats for more than 15 000 spectators can be added to an embankment.

The extended grandstand sweeps over a surrounding earth wall and gives a clear view towards the swimming pools. In the final analysis, this increases the original capacity from 4000 to 12000 spectators. Like the neighbouring Sydney International Athletic Centre, the Aquatic Centre gives priority to immediacy and intimacy of spectating, and uses an architectural language which is developed out of the Australian landscape.

The boulevard ends in the south near an industrial park and a multitude of smaller buildings, among them the State Hockey Centre (Ancher, Mortlock, Woolley) and the NSW Tennis Centre (Bligh, Voller, Nield) with 16 courts, one of the first rotunda stadia for 11 000 spectators.

In front of it is the Sydney International Athletic Centre which represents a new high point in the integration of form, function and landscape in Australian sports architecture. Forming a triad with the solid 'Australia Stadium' and the Aquatic Centre, it was used as the main competition arena (more than 15 000 seats) in conjunction with a warm-up track. An underground tunnel connected the International Athletic Centre with the 'Australia Stadium'. As a result, the building not only served as a competition site, but also as a warm-up arena for the Olympic athletes.

The Sydney International Athletic Centre does not burden the visitor with aggressive construction components or by off-the-scale dimensions. The curved main grandstand with its refined, innovative dome roof reinforced by wire cable and two steel framework poles forms a dynamic, visual counterpoint to the structures joined to the ground, located at eye level. The roof of the grandstand slopes forward, and a strengthening wire cable over the entire length absorbs the forces of the ascending air current.

The Sydney International Athletic Centre unifies aesthetics and practical usability – its effect is heightened even more by the charming hilly landscape, inspired by 'Aboriginal Dreamtime trails'. Sydney 2000 was praised by long-jumper, Heike Dreschler, as the 'loveliest Olympic Games town since Münich in 1972' – a synthesis of architecture and sport.

Werner Sobek

Retractable Roof over the Centre Court at Rothenbaum
Germany – Hamburg

Around 1892, the first German international tennis championships were hosted in Hamburg. If, at the beginning, it was still a pleasurable pastime and the preserve of rich business people and members of the aristocracy, since 1969, when pros were allowed on to the Rothenbaum centre court in Hamburg for the first time, it has become a mass business catering for an immense public.

The economic pressure to present matches on television without any of the contraints normally imposed by the weather, without games cancellations and stoppages, and with guaranteed planning and broadcast, led to the decision to install a roof over the centre court. The retractable, membranous roof construction completed in 1997 was designed by Werner Sobek and, with a span of 102 metres, is ranked as one of the largest retractable roofs in the world. The grandstand enclosure situated under the roof was renovated and functions as a sculptural object.

Werner Sobek's idea encompasses a light canopy – similar in form to a tent – whose conception is in line with the Olympic Games stadium in Münich (1972) by Günter Behnisch and Frei Otto, as well as the Roman Colosseum that was roofed over by white, textile awnings.

For Werner Sobek, it is about more than the 'changing motif'; his structure is comparable to an umbrella which unfurls and, when opened, forms a completely taut surface over a filigree, flexible rod structure.

Werner Sobek addresses the conventional image of the static, constructed piece of architecture in the Rothenbaum centre court by designing a versatile, responsive piece of architecture which is related to the development of microelectronics and computer technology: a piece of architecture which could correspond to this develpment by means of changing construction – achieved by implementing lithe movements until an outside expanse changes into an interior (and vice versa).

The retractable roof of the Rothenbaum centre court is comparable to the reversed principle of the spring aperture of a camera. A flattened, domed form made from a PVC- coated polyester membrane can be gathered from the circumference to a central point, so that the interior of the centre court is opened up. When no more than the tightly folded cover is visible against the opened space in the centre, the transformation is complete. The usually sharp separation of building (roof) and space is at times no longer noticeable; the classic boundary between inside and outside is removed.

The aesthetic momentum of the translucent membrane amounts to the new spatial designation: in closed state and in artificial exposure, the circular, gently vaulted cover changes into a completely new, space-enhancing form. Comparable to a discus, the light-reflecting/light-absorbing area seems to hover over the grandstand enclosure.

Werner Sobek developed the mechanics, structure and cover so that the adaptable cover is able to react to climatic conditions. The spectators and observers of the centre court are faced with a new spatial-temporal experience. The path from volume to surface, from construction to information, is mapped out.

The roof takes on different meanings: folded/unfolded, information and information carrier. The switch from its function as a building component (a retractable architectural element) to a media-carrying tool is signalled.

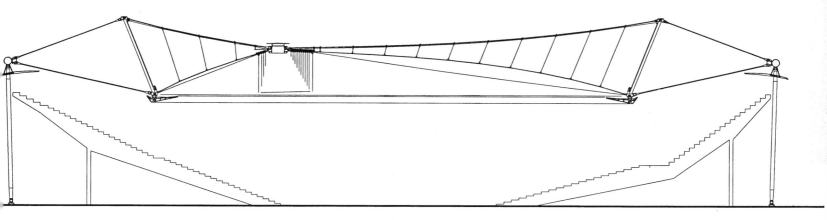

Cross-section of rope trusses 3 and 13
Scale 1 : 500

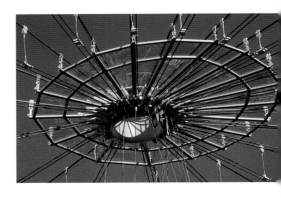

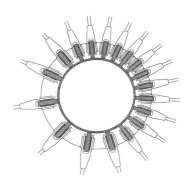

**Central knot
Sectional plane, top girder and
cable truss**

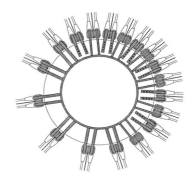

**Central knot
Sectional plane, lower girder and
cable truss**

The roof structure is derived from the construction principle of a
spoked wheel. An outer ring with a firmly anchored membrane
(also made from PVC-coated polyester material) offers protection
from the weather over the grandstand enclosure. Over the playing
field, the retractable inner roof is opened towards the middle, or it
is closed towards the outer ring.

The outer and inner roofs consist of two wheels which lie flat, and
are built inside one another on the same level. Corresponding to
the image of the spoked wheel, the spokes (steel cables) connect
the two outer pressure rings of the grandstand roof. Spokes (steel

**A trolley system is used in the central
knot. The number of trolleys is dependent
on the length of the cable truss.**

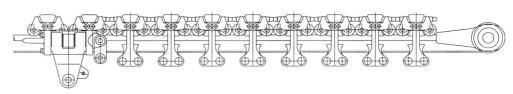

cables) also connect the inner pressure ring of the grandstand roof covering with the central hub. The spokes are spatially inserted, like the wheels of a bicycle. Curved columns stabilise the upper and lower spokes of the wheel.

The folding membrane of the inner roof is suspended from sliding trolleys which glide onto the lower spoke cables of the inner roof. In less than five minutes, the membrane is folded inwards – driven by electric motors – in the direction of the central hub, or is unfolded in the opposite direction. The movement is operated synchronously by hundreds of non-contact, measuring sensors, and reacts to various weather conditions. Electric motors operate hydraulic locking systems.

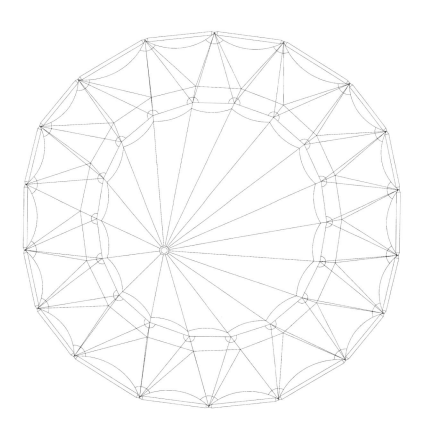

**Top view of the roof,
outer and inner membranous roof
scale 1 : 1 000**

The principle of the flat-lying spoked wheel had already been tried out in the Stuttgart stadium (280 metre span, Jörg Schlaich, Rudolf Bergermann), and with the retractable roof covering for the Saragossa arena (88 metre diameter, Schlaich, Bergermann, Werner Sobek).

The character of Werner Sobek's roof construction is completely new: the roof is less an example of architecture than of a machine normally used in mechanical engineering, but here transformed by electric power and feedback control technology.

Following its conversion into an exercise area for athletes and spectators, the Rothenbaum centre court can face new challenges intelligently, its retractable roof adaptable, and reacting to changing weather conditions with electric motors.

As if the retractable roof of the centre court were the transition from the mechanical world of the industrial age to the era of electronic media, Werner Sobek developed a hybrid structure. It comprises highly developed movement mechanics and control techniques used in modern mechanical engineering, plus the advanced development of long-reaching structures with minimal weight and material, together with convertible, folding surface modelling.

Henri and Bruno Gaudin

Stade Charléty
France – Paris

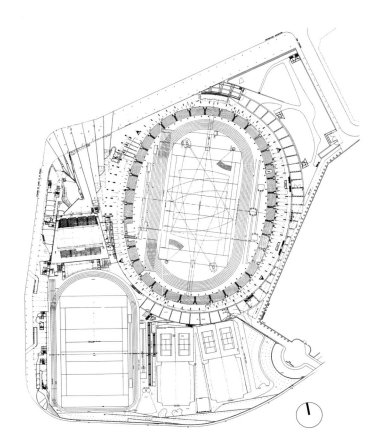

Site plan, scale 1 : 5 000

Building provides an outlook for the future. Independent of this, the ancient world had a determining influence on Henri and Bruno Gaudin's concept for the Charléty stadium in Paris: the arena which opens itself out to city life, and connects sport and the city with each other. The result is a piece of architecture characterised by fluid space which, in spite of the expanding open country, integrates the metropolis of Paris and constructs a form of communication between the open space and the large dimensions of the sports site.

It is indisputable that the purpose of buildings is derived from their interrelation with the city, and that they establish their existence with this precondition. As a 'Cité des Sports' situated on the not-so-attractive outskirts of the city in the north-east of Paris, next to the Boulevard périphérique, the Stade Charléty makes a reference to the countryside of the Vallée de la Bièvre, the hills of the Kremlin Bicêtre, and the 13th Arrondissement with the high-rise buildings of the Quartier d'Italie – and this it does simultaneously.

The urban dimension of the Gaudin concept – opening out towards the city of Paris, and the transparent airiness of the stadium – contrast sharply with the achievement-oriented mental focus of the athlete, if not of the audience itself, and would represent their interrelation as a microcosm of city life. The sin of speculation is atoned for.

From its intended function as a sporting tool, the 'Cité des Sports' which opened in 1994 has become a meeting place for city people through sport (track and field athletics, tennis, judo and squash among others), and through expanded usage (flats and offices) in an interconnected structural ensemble. Isn't this the most important message to have come from Pierre de Coubertin in the less than one hundred years since the first modern Olympic Games?

The roof structure is suspended above the V-supports (reinforced concrete). Horizontal *vierendeel* ring struts stabilise the steel construction of the roof. The upper stands made from sheet-steel flange out of the V-support and are encircled completely by a *vierendeel* girder.

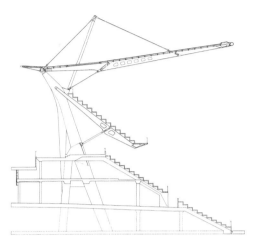

Section through the grandstand
Scale 1 : 500

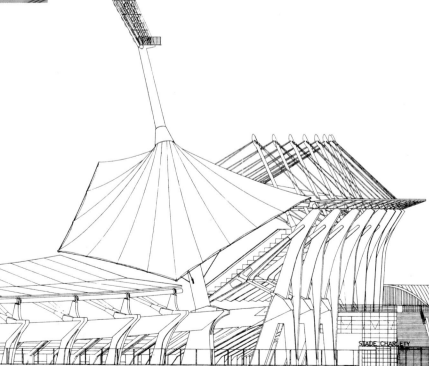

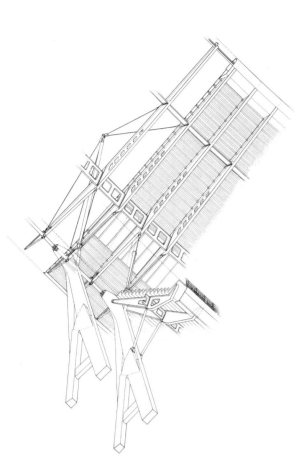

The striking, constructive presence of the large form of the stadium is legible, intelligible, expressive and stimulates the imagination – images reminiscent of skeletons, insects and organic objects. The wide expanse of the building which opens upwards is neither a playing field nor a park and nonetheless a public area. The void reserved for the dynamism of the human body, and the sheltered stands for the spectators stand in dialectical dependency.

The various forms of the buildings and the chosen materials relate to their individual uses. Ash-grey metal roofs meet roughened grey marble and black granite floors. Polished wall sections made from marble alternate with white-painted steel façades, and dominating white steel masts. The filigree reinforced concrete of the roof structure stands in contrast to the light, white polyester fabrics of the quasi-maritime awning.

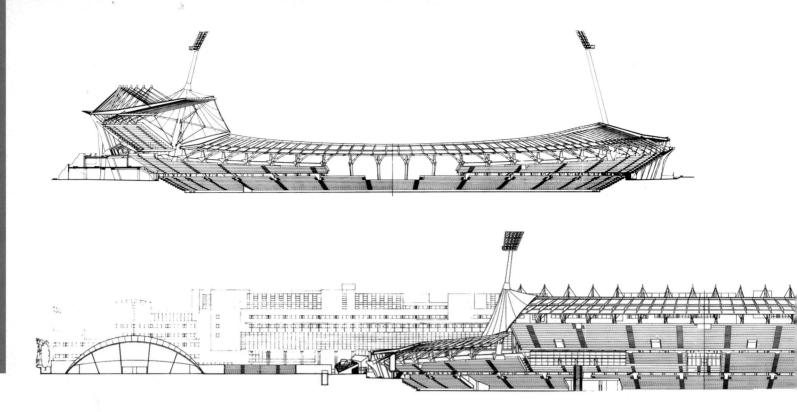

The 50 metre high steel mast of the floodlight installation acts as a mediator between the stadium and the Maison du Sport Français with the buildings of the Paris Université Club and the Comité Olympique.
Scale 1 : 1 250

Even if the vocabulary of forms and prefabricated parts appears to be borrowed from seafaring, a message in grey arises through colour and texture in dialogue with the city of Paris.

The accompanying linear development with offices and flats is used, among others, by the French Olympic committee. Similar to the wing of an aeroplane, or even comparable to the bow of a ship, it follows the street layout, the boundary of which is marked by an area eight hectares in size. The linear theme is multiplied almost sketchily in the formulation of the façade. The acacia avenue of the street also supports this effect.

The aim of Henri and Bruno Gaudin to capture space and emptiness in the municipal context of Paris, to apply the concept of Charléty, and to realise them architecturally as a maritime emblem in the grey colour of the city, cancels out the effect of the solid mass of the city and the individual object.
Charléty is becoming part of the 'deep and complex poetry of the great assets of Paris' (Baudelaire).

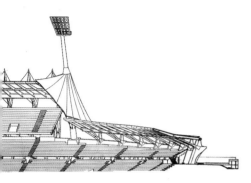

Philippe Chaix and Jean-Paul Morel

Stade de la Licorne
France – Amiens

The urban equilibrium of large cities – historic city centre, outskirts and surrounding towns – seems to be changing. On the one hand, it is the characteristics of the 'Global Village' which bring about far-reaching changes, on the other, it is those of small communities. The consequences can be seen in the awkward situation of the monotonous new housing estates located on the outskirts of European cities.

With dimensions comparable to those of cruise ships, centres catering for the growing requirements of free time, entertainment and sport (urban entertainment centres) are rising up on the outskirts of towns. Yet if there are social problems or riots, the 'lifeboats' are missing from these large 'steamers'. Reports on catastrophes in stadia (Heysel, Belgium) are growing in number. Sport no longer acts as a unifying force, but rather and increasingly as a polarising one. The reasons for this are gentrification and commercialisation, the split from the urban scene and the emotional volatility of a rapidly growing public.

Supply and demand of big events are on the increase; a developmental phase for stadia, entertainment centres and large-capacity sports halls is clearly recognisable. The experiences of the last few years led to the sports stadia and leisure facilities built in the 1990s being designed and checked particularly carefully with regard to safety.

The football stadium in Amiens is recognised as an undisputed and sophisticated triad of architecture, spectators and sport. Philippe Chaix and Jean-Paul Morel built the stadium on former marshland in an extensive area left to nature situated to the east of Amiens. The stadium with its orientation towards the town of Amiens with its Gothic Notre-Dame cathedral, and the tower house of Auguste Perret within view, as well as to the countryside of the Somme valley and the skies of Picardie, forms the starting point of planning.

Stade de la Licorne: the perfectly dematerialised glass cover looks out onto the town. Depending on changes in light, the stadium appears to be twinkling, transparent or translucent, and creates the effect of either proximity or distance to the town.

The effect of an extensive area opening upwards is reinforced by the glass cover, 26 metres in height, which curves in over the sides of the four stands – forming both a wind-protecting wall and a rainproof roof. Slender, flanging steel arches support the weight of the glass cover and withstand the force of the wind. At no time does the visitor feel claustrophobic as the glazed canopy of the stands keeps the corners clear and provides a view of the scenic surroundings. Under the glass cover, the visitor feels secure rather than confined.

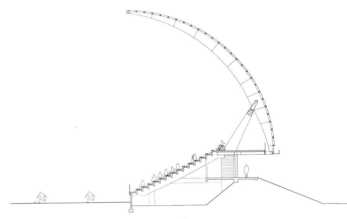

Cross-section, scale 1 : 500

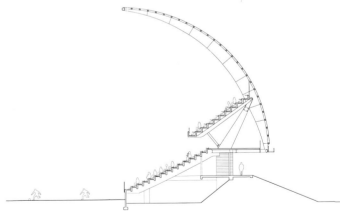

**Cross-section with stand enlarged by 800 seats
scale 1 : 500**

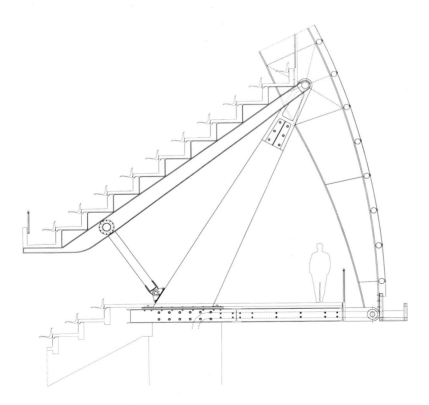

**Enlarged stand, cross-section detail
scale 1 : 100**

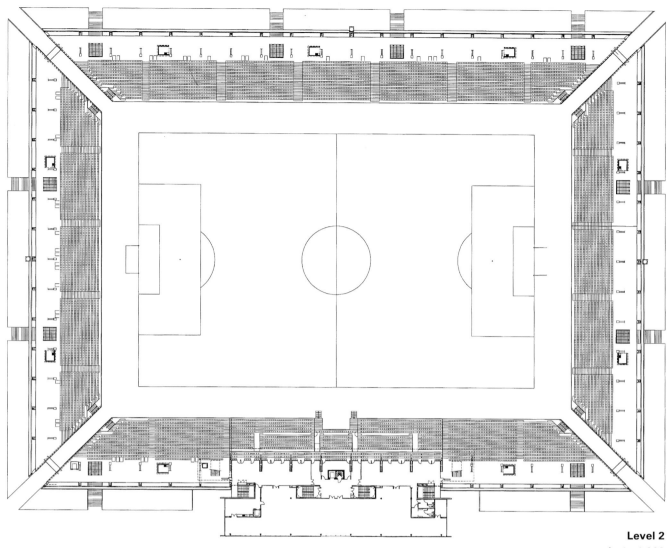

Level 2
scale 1 : 1 000

The glass roof made from 2 x 6 centimetres of laminated safety glass (aluminium-pressed strips and EPDM rubber profile) protects against the wind and rain. The lights at the upper end of the roof ensure that the stadium shines brightly in the evening.

The tight rectangle of the four constructed stands, which are situated closely around the football pitch, forms a direct spatial proximity between the 12 000 spectators and the players.

From outside, the stadium is viewed as an almost suspended, transparent construction, similar to a zeppelin that has just landed. A gentle bank of earth around the stadium reinforces the impression of the lightness of the glass cover. The slender quadrants made from steel-reinforced concrete which support the weight of the roof give the illusion of space.

The vast expanse of glass becomes a white spectacle of light in the evening, when the artificial lights turn the stadium into a crystal glass ship. Seen from Amiens and the newly built A16 motorway, a fascinating sight unfolds at night.

The geometry of the stands is laid down parallel to the edge of the playing field; just as simple and effective are the four entrances positioned at the same level in the corners of the stand. The spectators are led to the tower gallery which opens out towards the countryside, and from there they can reach the reinforced concrete stands, condensed into eight sections, above and below. Below the stands is the refreshment area as well as other facilities. A building on the west side is reserved for privileged spectators, the press and television. In a subsequent construction phase it is planned to increase the number of seats from 12 000 to 20 000 through the installation of additional galleries.

The scenic character of the stadium surroundings is highlighted as a central theme by heat-absorbing rows of trees positioned in a north–south direction. Provision has been made for 11 800 parking spaces and the open streets are covered over, of course. Intentionally, or for financial reasons, the rows peter out into the expanse of the countryside.

The welded, curved steel girders (made from flat-bar steel, ranging in height from 400 to 1400 millimetres) are joined minimally at the upper end by means of a steel tube (diameter – 355 millimetres).

Tony Garnier/Albert Constantin

Stade de Gerland
France – Lyons

In the ideal plan of a modern industrial city, the Lyons architect, Tony Garnier's (1869 – 1948), 'Cité Industrielle' is sketched as a spacious sports stadium for its 35 000 inhabitants. As if they were a separate urban organism, stadia have been structured since early times in streets, paths and stairs, enclosed by walls and partitions. Even the spectator forms an equal component of the events; in a crowd, he/she is part of an organised entity.

Tony Garnier's 'Cité Industrielle' of 1904/1917 pursues objectives of social reform: habitation, work and leisure time are to be bound tightly together. Not far from leafy suburbs, blast furnaces and shipyards dominate the cityscape. According to Tony Garnier, for the industrially ordered society, placing an elegant town house next to the stadium is to display the cultural splendour of the ideal city.

The stadium of the 'Cité Industrielle', with a 500-metre running track, a 666-metre cycling track, and a stand made out of reinforced concrete was developed by Tony Garnier for the city of Lyons, and completed in 1926. The well-proportioned, large-scale construction, opened out towards the city of Lyons, is respectfully assigned to the early modern age in France, and is recognised worldwide as an architectural cultural monument.

Rigorous structural requirements for the World Cup in 1998 which was also held in Lyons led to the conversion of the Garnier classic under critical, international scrutiny. Albert Constantin, the architect of the conversion, achieved a convincing result.

Scale 1 : 1500

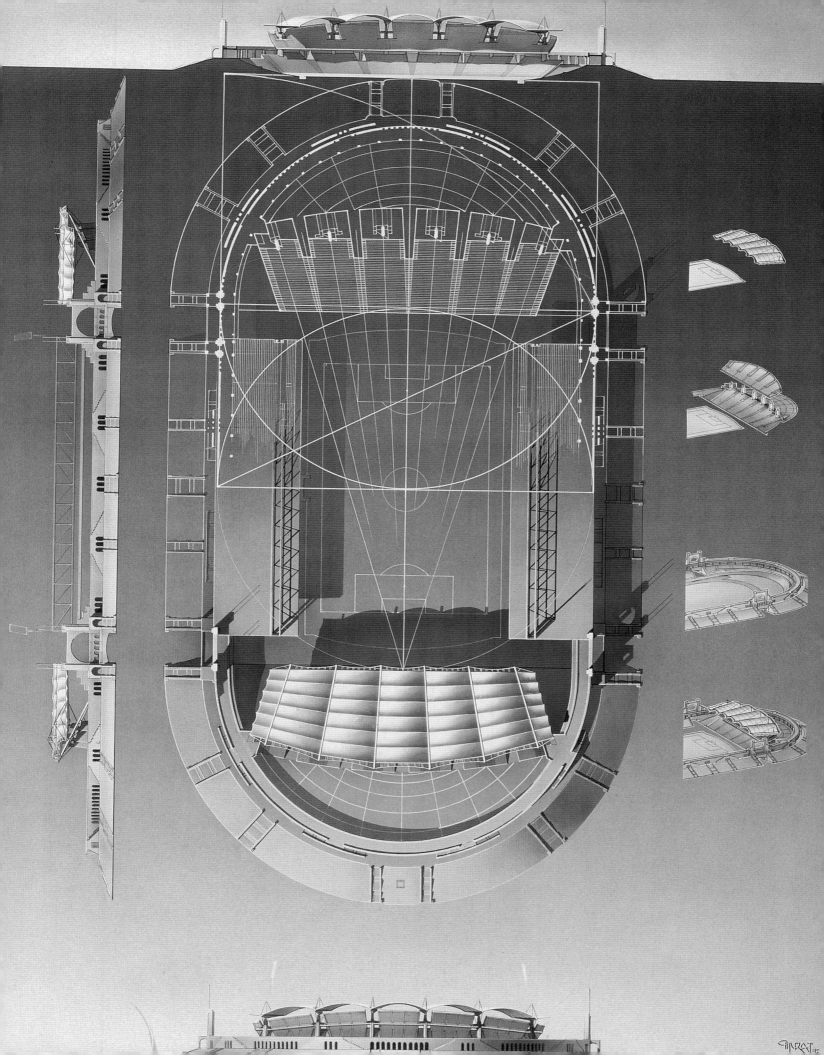

The rediscovery of the large form by Tony Garnier, designed proportionally in accordance with the golden section, is the starting point for Albert Constantin's careful metamorphosis of the historic Garnier stadium into a football stadium.

Of the 43 000 grandstand seats in the north and south curve, 16 000 acquired a rainproof roof made from light steel and textiles. The additional stands were planned in the horizontal projection and section, on the basis of Tony Garnier's original proportional calculations. At the same time, Constantin had some parts of the building, which had been added in the last few decades, and individual subsidiary buildings, removed. No more than that.

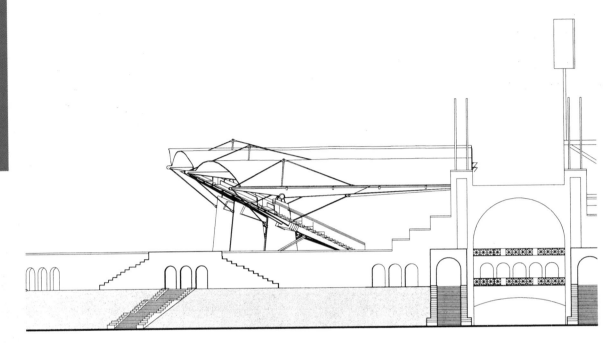

**View
scale 1 : 500**

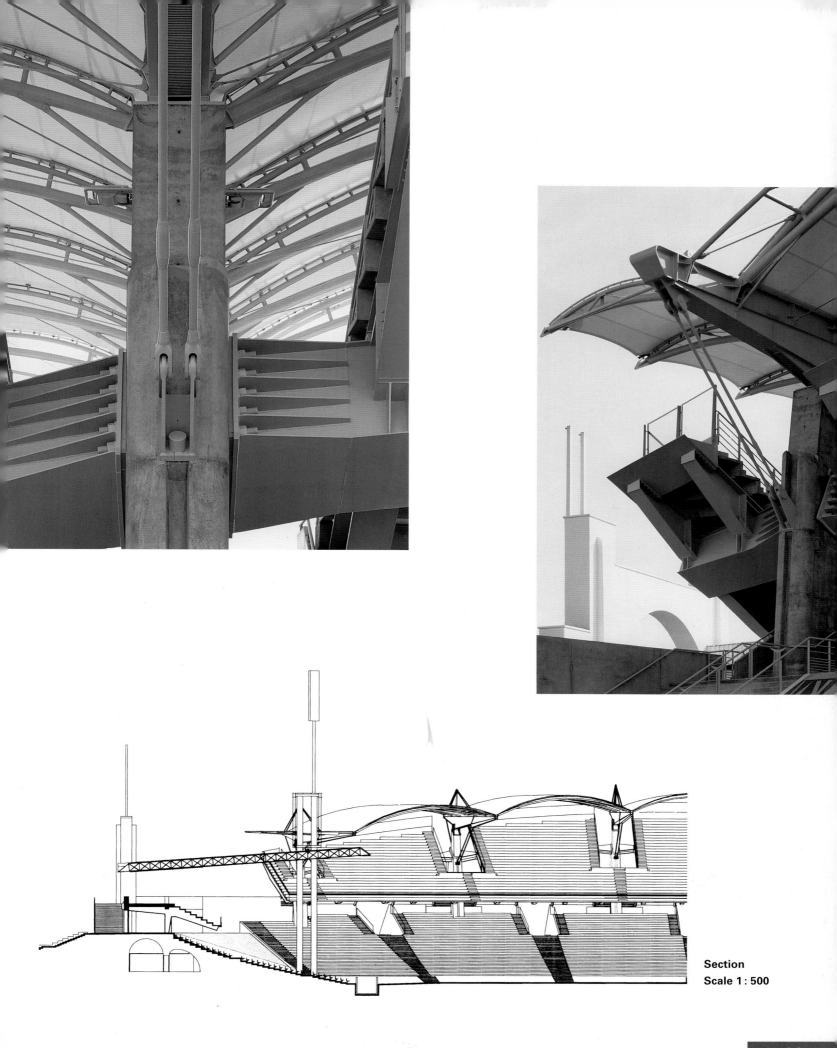

Section
Scale 1 : 500

New, lightweight stands of the north and south curves, made from reinforced concrete with textile roof covers covered with polyester, are aesthetically bound together with Tony Garnier's original structure (1913 – 1926).

The plinth of the stands, which hitherto formed the solid sculptural reinforced concrete boundary all around the playing field, remained as Garnier designed it with angular incisions at tight intervals, visually permeable to the inside and to the outside.

The scaffolding of the new roof cover over the stand and its weather-protective textile membrane appear as if suspended and form a lightweight contrast to the heaviness of the plinth of the stands.

The spatial and material transparency of the original Garnier stadium is retained. Experiencing the fascinating panorama and the atmosphere of the city of Lyons – the essence of Tony Garnier's architectural concept – this is something Albert Constantin was able to strengthen yet further through form and content.

The Stade de Gerland stands like a signal and focus in the big-city context of our times. Without detracting from the harmony of the original building, which still casts its spell over the spectators, Albert Constantin's design for the extensive new grandstand site rediscovers the rationale and constructive spirit of Tony Garnier.

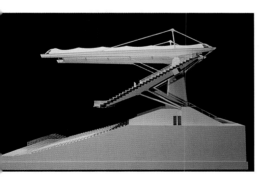

Renzo Piano Building Workshop

San Nicola Sports Stadium
Italy – Bari

Right at the beginning of the development of perspective during the Renaissance, the Italian 'Quattrocentro', which at the time, influenced buildings, squares and city spaces: the geometric game served the perfect image created by the upper classes, and aroused the citizen's interest in perception. The grand stadia which were constructed largely symmetrically and with equal sides for football and athletics, still rank among the last relics of this epoch.

Renzo Piano carried on the conceptual tradition of these buildings in Bari, and developed a football, track and field athletics stadium which is monumental both in terms of design and construction. The stadium can hold 60 000 spectators, but in spite of its size is nevertheless perceived as being people- and environmentally-oriented.

View, scale 1 : 2 000

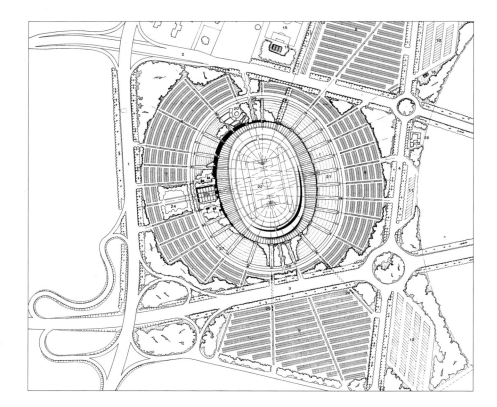

Site plan, scale 1 : 10 000

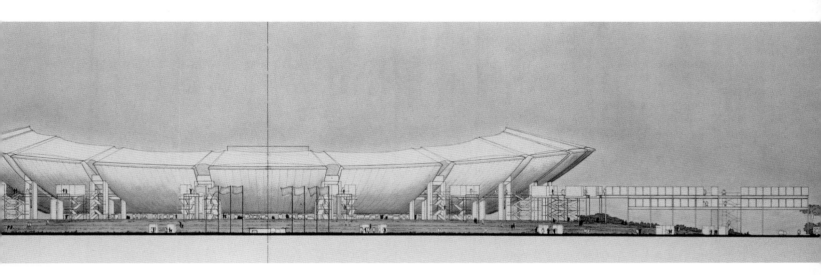

Renzo Piano combines the properties of techniques, materials and fine craftsmanship with a feel for Apulia's abundance of scenic beauties and its Mediterranean vegetation. In the last few years, the architectural biography of Renzo Piano has presented a series of significant icons, memorable and striking in structure, form and detail. The following rank among his best international pieces: the Centre Pompidou in Paris, the Beyeler-Museum in Basle and the Cité Internationale in Lyons as big-city interventions; or Kansai Airport in the Bay of Osaka and the cultural centre Jean-Marie Tjibaou in Nouméa, New Caledonia as countryside-oriented projects.

Peter Rice, who planned the stadium structure, describes the design which was realised for the World Cup in 1992, as a 'circular spaceship'. The spatial tension between the volume of the stands and the emptiness of the sports area, as well as between the sculptural construction and the flat geometry of the sports field is characteristic of Renzo Piano's concept. At the same time, there is the contrast between the stability of form of the construction, the pattern of the surrounding landscape, and the dynamism of the frequently electric atmosphere generated by the sporting events.

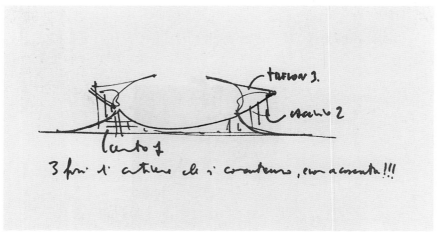

The safety of the 'spaceship' – obtained by a 26-axial radial system for 60 000 spectators – takes priority. In an architectural gesture synchronised with the rhythm of the construction, 8 metre wide entrances set between the 26 sections separate the spectators into well-defined blocks.

In the style of a Greek theatre, the sports area is sunk deep into the landscape, a concept that could also be compared to the crater of a volcano. The open, circular tower gallery of the stands, and the construction set above it to take the stands situated higher up, can be seen even from a long way off.

Organised into 26 entrances and 26 roofing segments, the sculptural impact is increased when lit up at night.

The impression of a spaceship is reinforced by the translucent roof cover of the circular stand with Teflon™ strengthened by fibreglass.

The lighting system is installed at the top of the concave roof cover of the stands. When lit up at night, the stadium appears like a mysterious space object, or a poetically alien flower.

With regard to scale and production, Renzo Piano refers to the Castel del Monte, the chiselled stone hunting lodge of the Hohenstaufens. Just as the hunting lodge rises monolithically above the plateaus and gently rolling hills of Apulia – structurally bound and yet, at the same time, opened up to the countryside through its skilful window arrangement – Renzo Piano sees the stadium in a sculptural dialogue, tightly bound to the landscape and the structural context.

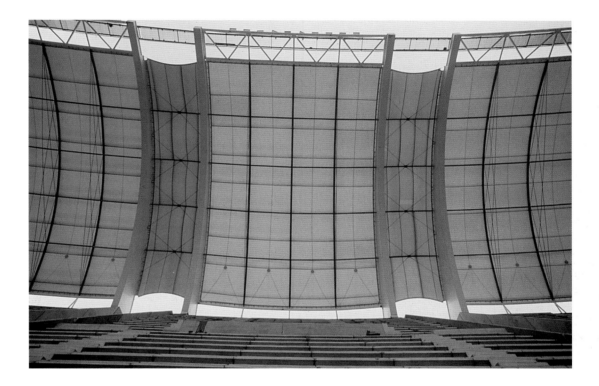

The San Nicola Stadium presents itself as a dynamic form which takes into consideration such fundamental aspects as:
– visibility
– environmental conditions and
– safety requirements.
By means of aerodynamic experiments in the wind-tunnel, the environmental conditions have been investigated both inside and outside the stadium. Formation of air pockets on the playing field is avoided when the distance between the edges of the stand roof is more than four times that of the height. Overheating on the stands is prevented by placing openings which are one to one-and-a-half metres in size, at the back of the stands. The experimental method of establishing a form for the ground plan and section is verified by computer-based, mathematical tests.

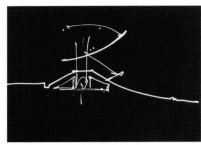

A sketch by Renzo Piano for the 'promenade architecturale' situated at ground level and positioned in the sloping hill. The upper stands can be found above it, the lower stands and facilities are dug into the hill.

Each stand has its own entrance so that the spectator's ability to see and move is not restricted. Double separation: horizontally, between the upper and lower tiers of the stand; and vertically, through 26 cuts in the oval of the stadium. The lower stands work like a crater, around the edge of which are the individual 'petals'. The separate concrete shells of the 'petals' are produced as unified elements on site from reinforced concrete. Each sector is held up by four supports made from reinforced concrete. The service area (sanitary facilities and changing rooms) can be found in the substructure.

Scale 1 : 250

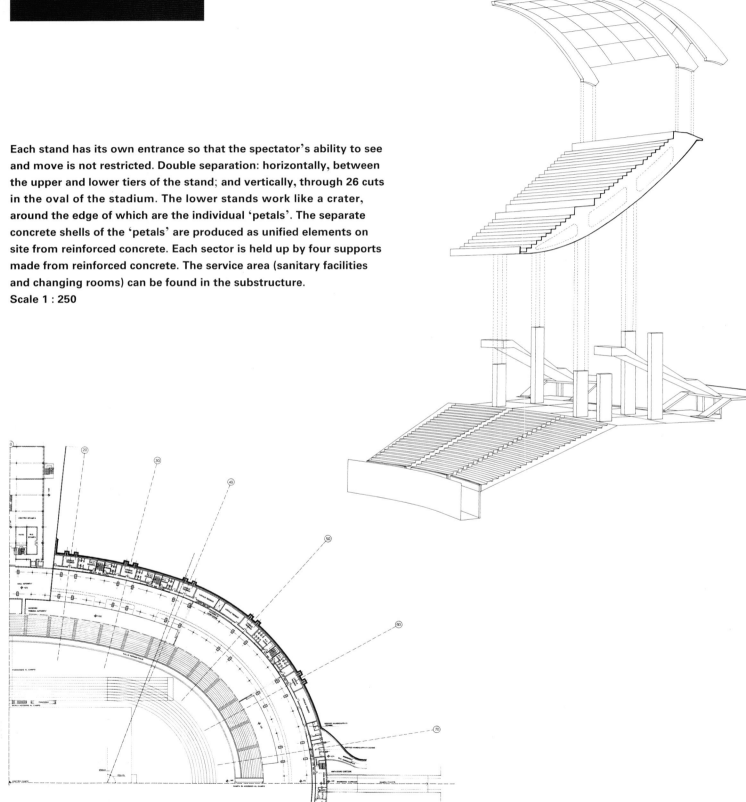

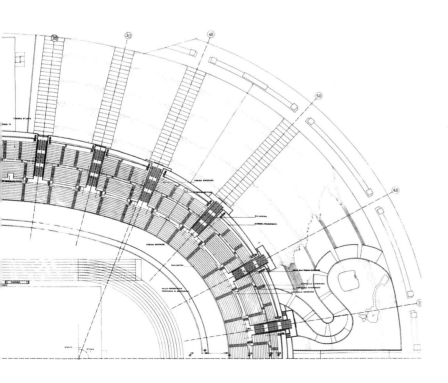

The clear, geometric form of the stand construction made from prefabricated parts of reinforced concrete, and of the roof made from a translucent membrane, are fundamental to developing controlled climate conditions in the stadium. The aims of this are to prevent overheating in the spectator blocks, as well as bothersome wind movement in the stadium. The ratio of total length to total height of the stadium had to be calculated so that no wind turbulence could occur on the playing field. In addition, it is also vital to obtain a constant exchange of air in the warmer season by means of a transverse ventilation system. The buoyancy force of the wind was also determined at the stadium in Bari in order to stabilise the edges by means of additional structural elements, similar to the landing flaps of an aeroplane. The conception and calculation outcomes were examined in the wind-tunnel.

The white, translucent, heat- and sunlight-reflecting material of the roof cover gives the stadium a balanced and harmonious effect. Moreover, as a requirement for high-quality HDTV broadcasts, the membrane reduces the brightness contrast between the uncovered playing field area and the closed stand constructions; the 1992 World Cup was held in Bari's San Nicola stadium, designed by Renzo Piano, in front of an enormous crowd of spectators.

Michael Alder

Rankhof Football Stadium
Switzerland – Basle

As if the meaning of simplicity were self-evident, Karl Popper defines it thus: 'If we follow the modern interpretation, "simple" denotes the reduction to the essential and the comprehensible.' 'Simple' concerns sense and expression, and not stylistic purity or Protestant ethos. And Hermann Finsterlin elevates the perception-wise order – already anticipated for our epoch by Plato or Goethe – to a cosmic dimension: '... and the day will come when the great Simple will dawn anew, with its everlasting calmness, the highest of all, an enhancement of reality which we can just imagine'. The following quote is accredited to Einstein, '... we are to make everything as simple as possible, but not simpler'.

Simplicity does not exclude complexity; in essence, it involves the establishment of a balance: between information and reduction (of aesthetics), or between complexity and simplicity (of the construction).

Deciphering the local conditions of the Rankhof stadium was Michael Alder's first step from complexity to simplicity. The Rankhof stadium is part of a narrow sports area with 16 sports fields lined up along a concentric path squeezed into a small area shared by more than ten small Basle clubs. A distinct micro-society with its traditional club life has emerged here over the last 70 years. The restricted space is explained by the noticeable concentration of traffic from the Swiss-German-French Basle region. The site itself is situated between the bank of the Rhine to the east, a railway embankment to the north, railway lines to the west, and a road to the south.

Michael Alder deliberately sought a simple and land-saving solution for building over the concentric development path, which also had to be achieved at low construction costs. The slender grandstand (1000 seats) is stacked above an equally long hall in order to create an 'urban vessel' (Michael Alder) for sport and club activities. In the lowest section, various facilities and function rooms cater for the stadium. The playing field is contained vessel-like on the remaining sides by steps which can be used for sitting on, so that the connections strived for by Michael Alder with the role models from antiquity (gymnasia, amphitheatres) emerge in an almost ceremonial way.

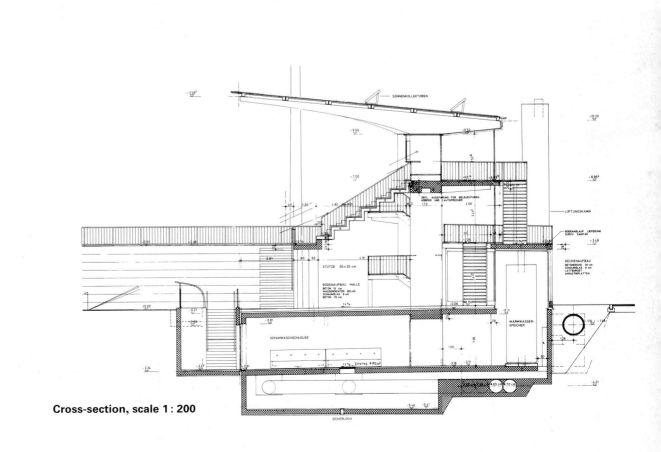

Cross-section, scale 1 : 200

Perhaps it is the cost constraints which, by reducing the construction methods (pre-fabricated parts made from reinforced concrete without a covering layer, with tension safety measures to improve the tightness of the joints), demand simplicity in a pragmatic and aesthetic way. On the roof, a technical vacuum sucks away any rain, snow and ice, resulting in minimised construction here as well.

The plainness of the stand construction expresses both practical dignity and merry splendour – in a simplicity which can be traced back to geometry and order, or to the elementary structural essence. If it was necessary to develop the stadium in both a simple and complex way, then Michael Alder has convincingly succeeded in fulfilling the requirement of sport and the club life to go with it.

Hermann Tilke, Peter Wahl, Ulrich Merres

Sepang International Circuit
Malaysia – Sepang

After a terrific competition (8 months' planning, a 14-month construction period), Chairman Bernie Ecclestone assigned the Formula 1 privilege to the Malaysian Sepang International Circuit. The investment of the former amateur racing driver and architect, Hermann Tilke with Peter Wahl, Ulrich Merres (cost: 70 million euros) affords unbridled image promotion for the South-East Asian state.

On 18 April 1999, Michael Schumacher, the king of speed, who had broken his leg in an accident at Silverstone 14 weeks before, sped off from the start in the most exciting race of the season. The Ferrari double victory turned into a magnificent comeback. Then came the disqualification; however, the all-clear was given a few weeks later.

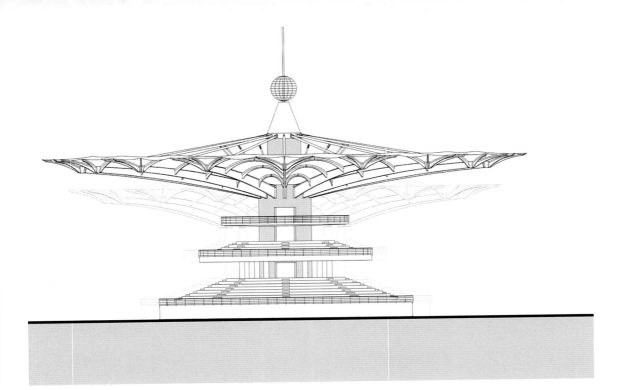

View
scale 1 : 500

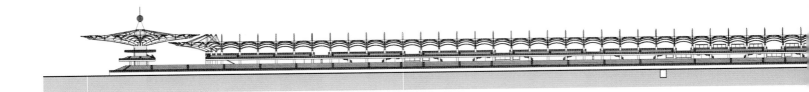

Back-to-back stands
scale 1 : 500

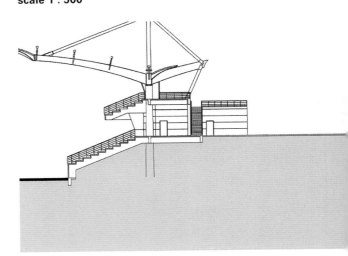

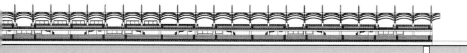

View, scale 1 : 2 000

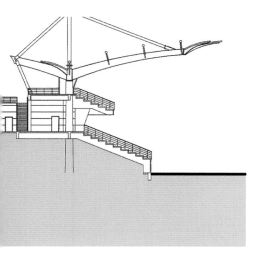

0   5   25m

Without heated hysteria and a cold shower, the ultramodern investment of the Aachen architects would be inconceivable. The aerodynamic innovations of the car correspond to the gently curved textile membranes above the spectator seats on the back-to-back stands, almost 600 metres in length from start to finish. Not only do the vehicles sparkle, the pavilion-like, glass driver camps (Pit Building) with pits and various facilities also gleam with glass, aluminium and polished steel. For the drivers, the track is a challenge, the 'track for the next century' (Eddie Jordan).

With the 'Multimedia Super Corridor' on the outskirts of Kuala Lumpur, the Petronas Twin Towers, a new airport, a mosque for 15 000 faithful, and the race track, Malaysia wants to demonstrate its development and progress. Even the 100 000 spectators are included in advertising new tourist destinations when there is action on the 5.5-kilometre long racetrack.

The aesthetics of the architecture correspond to the marketing image of Malaysia as a modern developed state. The aura of a modern economic structure is reflected in a Formula 1 racetrack whose main event is characterised by the individual entrance of the unpredictable racing cars (and their drivers), as well as the world-wide onslaught of the 'event society' – and this could be for each TV transmission.

The appearance of a sophisticated piece of architecture whose dimensions place the visitor in the centre is a piece of provocative staging. The roof forms adopted from nature, comparable to veined leaves, have a concrete, touchable and enduring quality, in spite of the structure's ambitious conception.

The myth of speed is deconstructed on three levels: the racing cars which can go at more than 300 kilometres an hour, the modernisation of Malaysia, and the aesthetically and functionally sophisticated architecture link three speeds to one ambitious starting-point.

The visitor may find the racing grounds of Sepang a paradoxical experience, be it as a turbulent 'noise machine' or – translated as a piece of architecture which blends with difficulty into a landscape belonging to one of the most beautiful islands in the world – a feeling of contentment, reminiscent of Greek stadia. Here, architecture is both amusing reading matter and the fantasy repertoire of the visitor, as well as stimulating entertainment. And last but not least: the high standard of the avant-garde construction of the racing car is happily complemented.

Livio Vacchini

Sports Hall
Switzerland – Losone

The austere architectural construction rises above a spacious green area, seemingly well protected and without any obvious means of access. From outside, the sports hall gives the visitor the impression of being like a room which turns inwards, which is concentrated exclusively on itself through its architecture and construction, as well as the chiaroscuro.

The interplay of art and architecture, the beauty of the construction, the harmony of its individual parts in a minimalistic severity: this places Livio Vacchini's work in an area of conflict which traces the line of development from antiquity to Battista Alberti, via Ludwig Mies van der Rohe right up to Mario Merz.

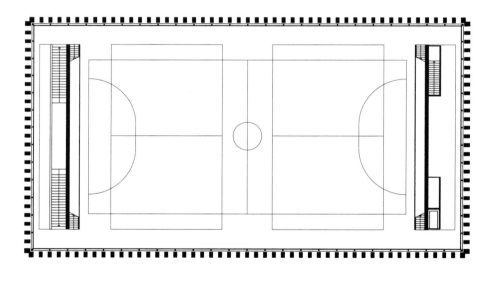

Scale 1 : 500

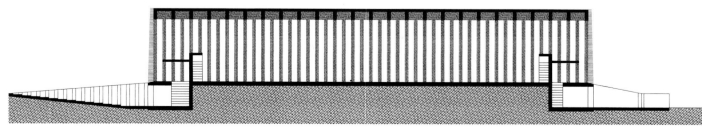

The sports hall of Losone serves a dual purpose in a particular way. In the midst of an otherwise closely guarded, military site, it is open to both the military employees and to the civilian public.

The establishment greets the visitor (the sportsman/sportswoman) in an environment imbued with peaceful harmony – yet nevertheless appears paradoxically inaccessible. On a long ramp constructed in front of the actual building, the path leads into the interior situated underneath. Exactly in contrast to the temple of antiquity whose steps led upwards and on which only priests were allowed to ascend, Vacchini leads the visitors over a mezzanine floor into the facilities floor below. Nevertheless, these facilities and changing rooms can be adequately lit naturally, as the hall level begins at a height of 1.4 metres, at just below eye level for the visitor coming in from outside.

From the facilities floor, two narrow flights of stairs lead up to the shorter sides of the rectangular hall which – free of all additional fittings – expresses nothing but its emptiness. Open to all sides in no particular direction, narrow window slits expose the room – as far as the structural engineering permits. The second time visitors look at it, they discover the complexity of the architectural aim here as well: rhythm, repetition, orientation in the horizontal room, and contact with the landscape.

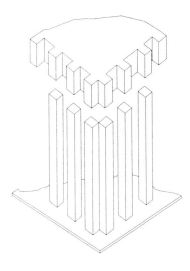

The harshness of the sharply cut light and shadow areas on the floor and on the walls of the hall strikes the visitor like entering a room in a film. The symmetrical order of the hall heightens the undisturbed effect of the film motif. Not until the visitor moves in a 'promenade architecturale' does the subtle balance of structure, space and scale of the building become apparent. This interaction of subject (visitor) and object pervades the architecture.

The inside of the reinforced steel roof, like the floor a light shade of yellow, dominates the muted stillness of the room. As a grill of girders at a height of 8.16 metres, the roof structure made from prestressed reinforced steel spans the total area of 56.50 x 31.64 metres support-free. Clearly recognisable from outside, the grill of girders only lends its support where the closely placed reinforced steel supports of the outer boundary can lift it up.

In order to show this attachment clearly, a barely noticeable joint separates the grill of girders of the roof structure from the outer supports. A break with the classical period? If the inspiration of the Doric temple of the ancient world is obvious, then Livio Vacchini does without the heaviness of the ceiling peripheral girder, the tympanum, which traditionally lies horizontally over the supports.

Scale 1 : 500

In a calculated reduction, he harks back to Ludwig Mies van der Rohe, who, as in his Seagram Building in New York, overrides the effect of the ceiling and roof segments in favour of traversing I-girders which are led outside in front of the space-enclosing glass exterior. Even superseding the ancient corner pillars by eliminating them – rather like Ludwig Mies van der Rohe – leads Vacchini to the creation of a 'frameless', and consequently, to an almost continuously active, outer wall.

The dimensions of the membrane-like inner glass façade – moved away from the tightly placed outer supports – are based on the 'modulus' by Le Corbusier. Introduced by Le Corbusier in its simplest sense as the relation of scale between the person and their surroundings, the 'modulus' obtains a basic proportion of 2.26 x 4.08 metres. Livio Vacchini integrates this in the height, width, and ground plan of the glass-enclosed sports hall.

In order to break the verticality of the reinforced steel supports which surround it from outside with this proportion of 1:1.180, the inner glass façade is horizontally incised at a height of 4.08 metres. The two glass bands, which are of equal height, are so situated that a varied pattern develops between the vertical partitions of the two glass bands, whose aim is to confuse the visitor. In the grid ceiling, at a height of 8.16 metres, the geometrically transformed façade partitions meet harmoniously once again.

The natural light that fills the room and – this is a positive experience from inside – is able to lift the division of inside and outside, initially giving the visitor the effect of a dignified, almost sacred atmosphere. Only when visitors set out on a 'promenade architecturale' do they experience the chiaroscuro pattern of the architecture and the construction elements as if they were cinematically intensified. A separate effect in terms of an exciting contrast is created by the encounter with the scenic natural surroundings.

For Livio Vacchini, the properties of the building are supposed to be only slightly predictable in terms of their impression on the visitor. They are in ironic interplay with the surprise of the visitor at the effective, unpredictable, architectural changes of the building, which nestles in a just as predetermined, yet constantly changing landscape.

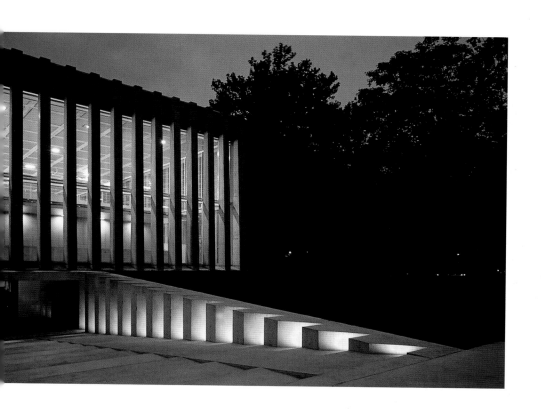

Stefan Camenzind and Michael Gräfensteiner

Buchholz Sports Hall
Switzerland – Uster

Meet a new generation of architects: two architects who have won international prizes and awards in just a few years present their 'first house' (Bauwelt prize, 1999) in which they broke new ground with a minimal approach and conceptional concentration. The judges of the Europe-wide competition see the sports hall as a testimonial to 'simplicity, as making the most of limited means, and designed for function rather than for design's sake'.

The unusual outcome of a triplex sports hall with seats for 1000 spectators is the result of an 'integral way of thinking and working' (Camenzind and Gräfensteiner). Each element of the sports hall is multifunctional. Conceptual clarity, constructive simplicity, cost-saving by limited usage of few component parts, and ease of orientation for its users are the main features of the sports hall in Uster.

Through the construction of transparent glazing (north and south side) and translucent façade elements (east and west side), the hall becomes bathed in daylight, even when the sun's rays are scarce. When the sports hall is illuminated at night, interior and exterior appear reversed.

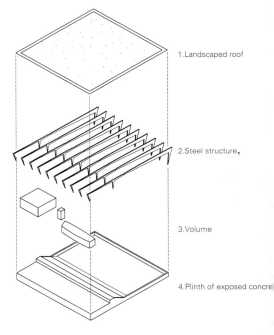

1. Landscaped roof

2. Steel structure,

3. Volume

4. Plinth of exposed concre

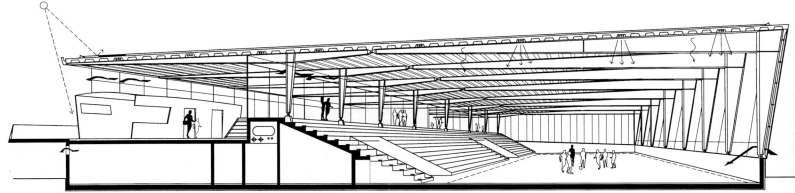

The southwards-projecting steel construction of the roof and material screen protect against solar radiation. The concrete construction of the plinth and the stands act as a storage compound and guarantee a cool room temperature, even in the height of summer.

A ramp on the south façade leads into the entrance area. Here we find a cash desk and kiosk, toilets, a room for administration, and a gymnasium. From the entrance area, the onlooker enters the stands of the sports hall with its 1000 seats. Telescopic stands are brought in during training. The exposed concrete plinth below the entrance hall is ideal for additional uses: equipment rooms, changing and shower rooms, storerooms and a technical department, as well as a small seminar room. A lift also suitable for the disabled connects the floors.

The steel construction of the roof complies with the minimal cubic profile. The translucently glazed east and west façades (made from light-dispersing insulated glass with a capillary plate insertion offering protection against the sun), and the transparent north and south façades ensure a dazzle-free, diffuse quality of light in the interior of the hall which is optimal for all kinds of sport.

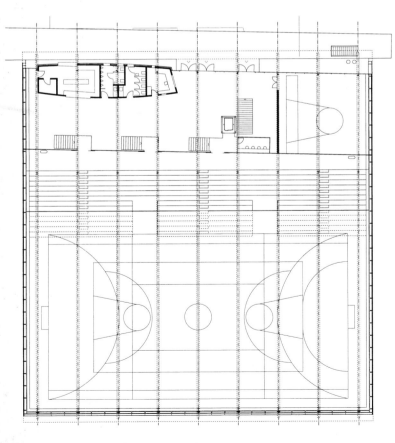
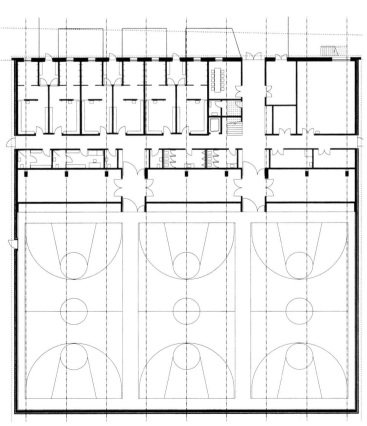

The superstructure seems to hover on the circular plinth. The form of the three welded hinge trusses in the roof and that of the cast-iron support hinge in the transition to the concrete plinth comply with structural engineering minima. The roof is shear, strengthened with a trapezoid covering visible on the inside and, thanks to its perforations and size, does not satisfy only the requirements of structural engineering. Acoustics, lighting and cover are integrated into the sheet metal trapezoid roof. The roof, rising to the north, is extensively landscaped.

The structure is easily read: remarkable lightness, elegance and efficiency of material. We witness here a hall of light, economical in construction, the result of careful planning and workmanship, and of a high architectural standard.

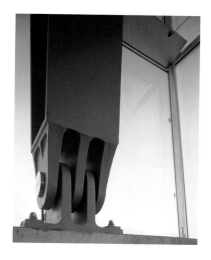

Scale 1 : 500

Peter Kulka

A Hall for Sport and Culture
Germany – Meiningen

Urban developmental and architectural concept

The district of Meiningen-Jerusalem is characterised by residential buildings constructed in a prefabricated style which surround a former industrial estate, parts of which have been reused. Jerusalem is in an attractive scenic location in the foothills of the hilly landscape of the Rhone, and at the start of the densely wooded areas of the Thuringian forest, some three kilometres from the historic town centre of Meiningen on a slope dropping down to the Verra valley. In contrast to the urban development – with its large-scale drawing-board designs for the housing estate on the northern side, and scattered small summerhouses on the south side of the valley – the heterogeneous requirement, the polarity of human needs and their architectural realisation are convincingly expressed.

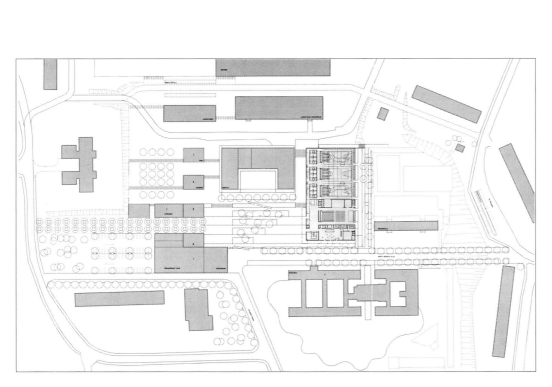

Site plan, scale 1 : 3 000

The urban developmental rigidity which is frequently apparent in other prefabricated housing estates is here broken by the sloping site and the delightful views onto the Verra valley. What was missing from the housing estate, as with so many other satellite towns, was a central area with the residential qualities of a public, urban space. In fact, existing public buildings, a grammar school, a primary school and administrative district buildings which could possibly be developed as a centre, were not connected in an urban development because of their isolation.

The design idea for the district centre of Meiningen-Jerusalem aims to enhance the status of the peripheral area of the district, to improve the infrastructure and to offer a place where people can interact in order to improve their public life. In the conversion, the theme expressed by the existing, rectangularly shaped buildings was picked up and reinforced by new buildings. A square was also built, with two converging avenues leading into it. The residential areas in the north and south are linked to each other for the convenience of pedestrians.

The avenue forms the backbone to the urban developmental ensemble and opens up possibilities for development for various uses: the north, the area designated for infrastructure and living – with services such as shops, businesses, pharmacies – and in the south, the school area with a grammar and primary school. In the middle of the district centre is the communication sector, which forms a lively area by means of playful swirling tree arrangements, and which contrasts with the basic orthogonal structure of the housing estate.

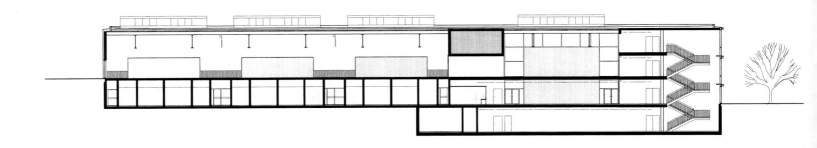

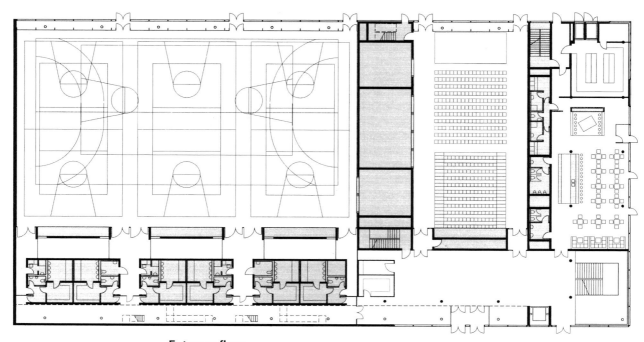

Entrance floor
scale 1 : 500

The terraced lay-out of the square and the avenue follows the natural topography and creates a connection between the existing and newly planned buildings. The new indoor building of the district centre forms a space-enhancing square border next to the buildings of the former commercial sector, now converted into the administrative district. The cube form of the hall relates to the strictly right-angled building structure of the surrounding residential building. A high canopy which – thanks to its dimensions – visually elevates the square, points at the main entrance.

The multifunctional hall consists of a hall with three courts, a multi-purpose hall and a leisure centre. In order to determine the dimensions of the building, the space and area programme is consulted, which lays down regulations and specifications for sports halls. The structure combines design and construction methods using steel and reinforced concrete. The steel is set in, comparable to the coloured wooden constructions of Japanese halls. The external layer of the cube alternates between the closed and glass façade. Grey fibre cement facings and aluminium elements blur to a dullness. Through the glass façade, rich colours glow from the inside.

Three-court hall

Partitioning curtains subdivide the large
sports hall in the northern section. This hall,
as well as being connected for 40 metres,
is used for school and club sports, and
competitions.

Up to 750 spectators can follow the events
from extending telescopic stands. The hall is
provided with daylight by both the building's
longitudinal façades and by ceiling fanlights.
Light-dispersing capillary insertions in the
insulated glass, and translucent awnings in
front of the façade which can be lowered,
protect the player from bothersome
reflections. An animated environment,
which highlights the pleasures of sport,
is achieved through the deployment of rich
colours.

Multi-purpose hall

Three-court hall

Multi-purpose hall

Rooms for changing in and for secondary uses separate the three-court hall from the adjacent multi-purpose room. It is designed as a single-field sports hall, and, as well as being used for sporting activities, can also accommodate small-scale cultural events or concerts. Warm materials and colours make the hall suitable for cultural events. The room accommodates 450 spectators in the stalls area and in the extending telescopic stands. For standing events such as pop concerts, the room is designed to hold a maximum of 1000 people. It can be blacked out from all sides; there is also a control room, a mobile stage, and a connection to the restaurant kitchen for catering purposes.

Entrance area

The entrance area situated just off the hall is opened by a glass façade in the direction of the square. A spectator gallery on the first floor which is connected to the entrance area and the sports hall via airspaces, becomes the inner promenade of the hall. The end of the self-supporting staircase made from reinforced concrete emerges towards the outer room, and links the hall to the leisure centre.

Leisure centre

A restaurant with 75 seats is visually separated from the 'guest garden', bordered by the plane trees on the avenue, by means of an extensive glass façade. On the first and second floors, a fitness-aerobic centre complete with sauna lures the visitor – a welcome offer. The building's numerous possible uses fulfil the requirement for a lively place with a varied inner life for anyone with cultural and sporting interests.

Langhof-Hänni-Meerstein

Horst-Korber Sports Centre
Germany – Berlin

After the fall of the Wall, Berlin was supposed to be converted into a sports metropolis; yet application to host the Olympic Games 2000 was inevitably rejected in favour of Sydney. Unfazed by this development, Berlin still forged ahead with construction of the velodrome and the swimming pool (both by Dominique Perrault), as well as the Max-Schmeling Hall by Dietz, Joppien and Joppien.

As a prelude to the new enthusiasm for sport seen as part of a new cultural development, Christoph Langhof Architects demonstrated quality architecture in Berlin with a sports hall for handball, hockey and volleyball linked to a sports hotel, service and administrative areas, situated at the edge of the 1938 Olympic Games stadium (Werner March). What's more, these are living proof that sports buildings do not have to be solely functional; but rather, they can make an architecturally sophisticated contribution to the environment.

The Horst-Korber Sports Centre is proof of the environmentally-sensitive integration of complex facilities into an existing forest landscape. Built around trees in a privileged site and at the same time dug into a slope, the sports centre would appear hidden if it were not for the slim, soaring tower of the sports hotel and the striking steel pylons of the roof structure.

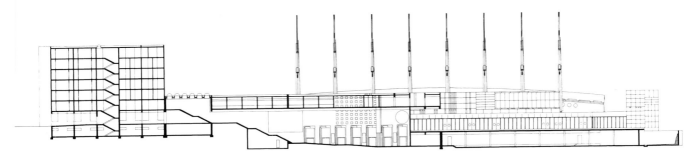

Longitudinal section: the sportsman's path from hotel to sports hall, changing rooms and power training gym

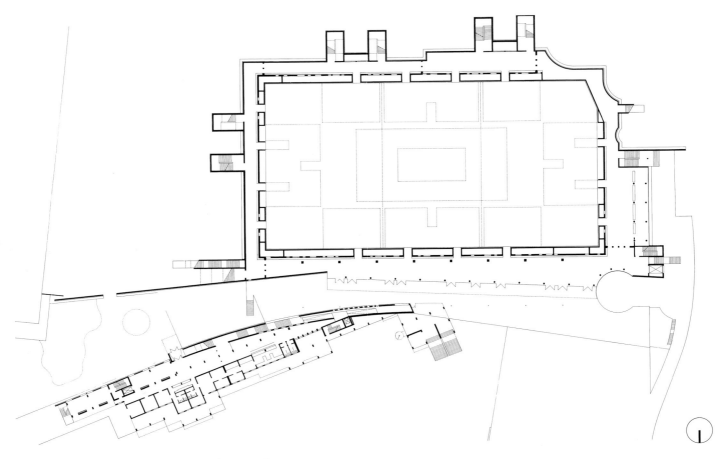

**Indoor level with spectator entrance, foyer and user entrance
scale 1 : 1 000**

The programme aims at top sporting performance: sportsmen and women make the greatest demands on themselves; for this purpose, next to the sports halls there are gyms for power training, re-energising pools, a sauna, facilities for sports medicine, training and seminar rooms, the seven-storey hotel with forty single bedrooms, a cafeteria and administrative facilities.

While for sportsmen and women there is a large-scale curved 'passageway into the depths' leading from the centre of the site with its cafeteria and other facilities, and which is made discreet from the south by means of small openings in the wall, for the spectators there are numerous entrances right around the sports hall. The spectator stands are located above the sports facilities.

The hall has many different uses. Although it is designed and constructed for handball, hockey and volleyball, other sporting events can also be watched. At 88.5 metres long, 45 metres wide and 14 metres high, the multi-purpose hall with a total capacity of 3450 spectators (accomodated on retractable stands) can be divided into as many as three individual halls, so that different events can take place at the same time but without impinging on one another.

The interior of the hall is both imaginative and aesthetically pleasing: sparse, wooden-planked walls enclose the interior from all sides. Above, the ceiling forms a dome of elaborate light movements in the gentle arch. Shimmeringly bright, with natural light provided by fanlights and 420 individual lights, the ceiling of light emphasises the quality of the high construction requirements.

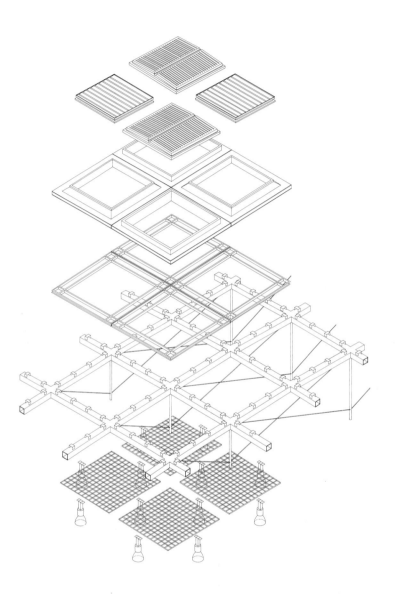

A self-supporting grating held underneath by steel cables and curved columns gives the impression that the roof floats on its slender dimensions. In the summer, the 4200 fanlights are opened so that people can play as if in the open air.

The transformation of the room is like a stage production when the spectator stands are extended from the wall by means of hydraulic power like a telescope, and lend the room a completely new character. Then, depending on the division of space 3450 spectators in a large multi-purpose room, or 2150 and 650 spectators at any one time in two rooms, or 1050, 650 and 475 spectators in three rooms, can follow a game or a competition simultaneously.

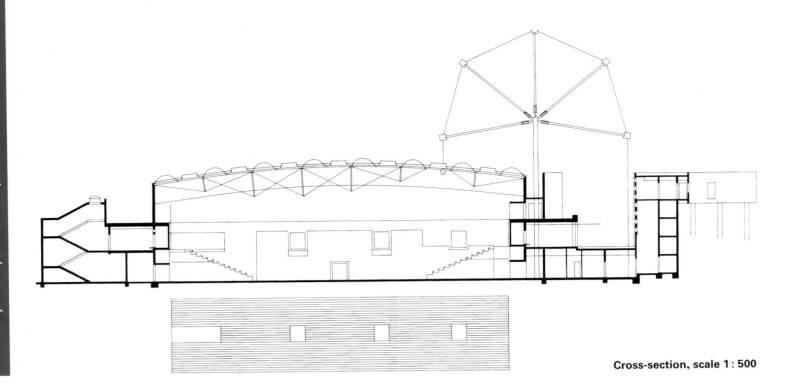

Cross-section, scale 1 : 500

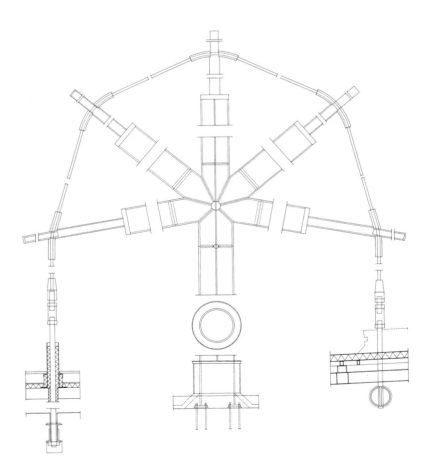

The steel construction of the roof structure hangs (in the first court) on cables which – spanning eight pylons – are anchored in the foundations.
Scale 1 : 250

Functioning as a landmark, eight pylons, 30 metres high, support the roof of the sports hall longitudinally. In visual succession with the treetops of the forest, they are a sign and benchmark for one's first visit. Step by step, the sports centre reveals the fineness of its construction and the highly developed detail of its architecture. The technical mastery with which the scenic integration, construction and materials moved from the industrial planning stage, and the way in which subtle, functional details present themselves to the sportsman and the spectator, becomes clear only on close observation.

With Christoph Langhof Architects, the sportman stands at the centre as a culture-conscious, sensitive and open-minded observer. For the sportsman or spectator brimming with expectation, the path to the sports grounds and to the spectator facilities is comparable to a 'promenade architecturale' in an atmosphere of subtle surprises.

Léon Wohlhage Wernik Architekten

Sports Hall in the Sixth Form College
Germany – Berlin

Classified as a historic monument, a symmetrical brick building by Ludwig Hoffmann dating back to 1912 and located in East Berlin is an extension to the sixth form college in the form of a totally plain building, clearly structured as a square stone block, and glazed with orange-coloured plaster. The self-assured and functional new building with a ground plan area of 30 x 57 metres, is connected only by an integrated glass bridge to the existing building, which houses the classrooms. The filigree suspension construction of the glass connecting passage reinforces the structural distance to the Wilhelmine school building.

The precise perforation of the windows and of the entrance, which is set back into the building, correspond to the severity of the box-like volume. Large expanses of wall and formats which have been cut out; the abstract interplay of opening and mass picks out the simple external architecture as a central theme whose internal spatial configuration is already decipherable in the composition of the four façades.

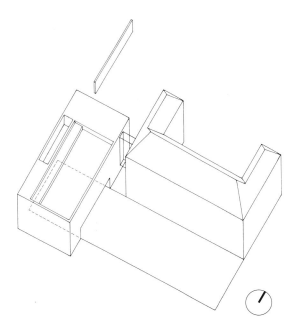

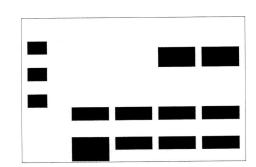

View of the southern side

View of the northern side, entrance hall of the sixth form business college
with footbridge between the new building and the old

View of the western side, scale 1 : 500

The canteen on the entrance floor, and the sports hall above the school administration offices create a spatial composition in the interior out of unequal volumes in the form of horizontally stacked spaces and wide halls, with steps, orientation points and exposed openings.

Movement becomes the permanent theme here. The interplay of large and small spaces, the great variety of complex material, detail and colour application, and the invitation provided by surprising openings urges movement with the aim of collecting visual experience from all the floors and all over, right into the outer room. The sparseness is expressed in the walls of the sports hall which are covered in yellow wooden material, in the canteen, made less severe by means of only a few coloured areas, in the wooden-glass doors, and in the light wooden and original asphalt floors. With patches of reinforced concrete, cracks in the form boards and bare steel girders, the stairwell and the sports hall blend into the decaying industrial buildings located in the surroundings of the sixth form college.

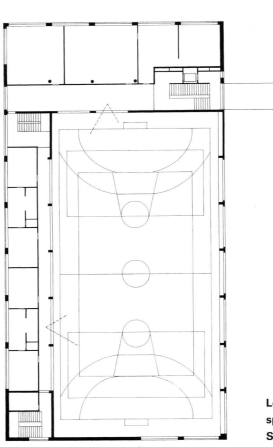

**Level 2 with
sports hall, changing rooms and specialist rooms
Scale 1 : 500**

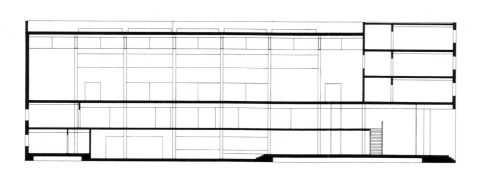

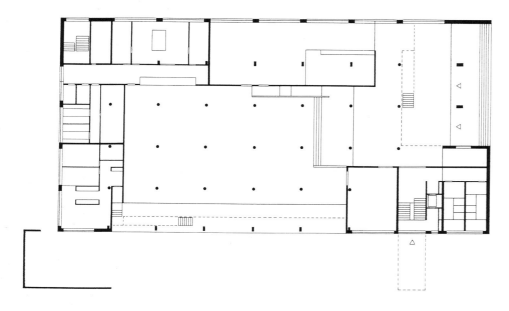

**Longitudinal section and ground plan
of the entrance level (level 0)
with canteen, kitchen and library
Scale 1 : 500**

The concept of a flexible set of corridors, of rhythmically free environmental planning, breaks away from conventional corridor ordering. The artist, Claudia Büttner, takes up the hole-in-the-wall principle of the outer façade and knocks irregular openings into the walls and a hole in the floor. The openings which have emerged – 'a longing for niches'– leave the view free for 'a longing for sights', for the view outside or into neighbouring rooms. The pupils are invited to take up the theme of 'a longing for sights' through videos which they have produced themselves, and their projection. Art as an opportunity with many possibilities has taken a step towards architecture.

The opposite standpoint to the New Baroque school building of Hoffmann carries a price: for public space, it is no good surrounding the complex inner rooms, with their unequal volume and internal composition directed outwards, with no more than minimalistic rationalism.

Vogel and Brunninger

Sports Facilities in a School for the Physically Disabled
Germany – Ingolstadt, in the 'Cavalier Elbracht'

When the physical and mental capabilities of someone at school are discussed, we soon get on to motor and mental handicaps and disabilities. Educationalists are divided about how best to cater for the less able-bodied. Supporters of integration argue with those in favour of special schools. Nevertheless, both sides are unanimous on the need to educate disabled children and provide as much physiotherapy as possible.

The discussion about what the optimal care of disabled people should involve is not over; there is to be no dispute – something which always exists with disability – over the fact that children and young adults should be socially integrated. This begins with paths and places in public areas being made easier to use for the disabled or for wheelchairs. The lowering of kerbs was one of the first requirements to have become standard practice. Yet it is still a positive exception when disabled people can use public transport without any problems, and, of course, are looked after in the process. Too many public and private buildings are still lacking in facilities adapted to the needs of the handicapped, which would make moving about easier for them.

The principle of not excluding disabled people is accepted everywhere. Even in a school environment, there are no ghettos. Countless examples prove that facilities for the less able are just as professionally planned as those for standard schools; sometimes they are even better, because the educational efforts in the planning phase are more intense and varied.

In Ingolstadt, the 'Cavalier Elbracht' where the sports facilities for the school for the physically disabled are housed, constitutes part of the second fortification, partially laid down by the architect, Leo von Klenze, in the nineteenth century, and which encircles the old town. In the houses named 'Cavalier', with 4-metre thick foundation walls, once guard patrols and soldiers were stationed. Today, these are the school's classrooms for the disabled.

Before that, in the so-called glacis, trenches – which were fully visible from the building – emerged from casements and ground ramparts. The fortifications were filled in due to the devastation caused by the Second World War. As in other cities, the fortifications formerly surrounded by ramparts and trenches are today integrated into the green areas of the inner city.

In order to preserve the park-like character of the rampart construction, the architects Vogel and Brunninger, who were awarded first prize in the competition, suggested uncovering the casements and placing the sports buildings for the existing school into the ground at a depth of 5 metres. Daylight is obtained via fanlights and the glazed areas of the halls, situated towards the fortification trench. They are connected underground to the existing main building of the school.

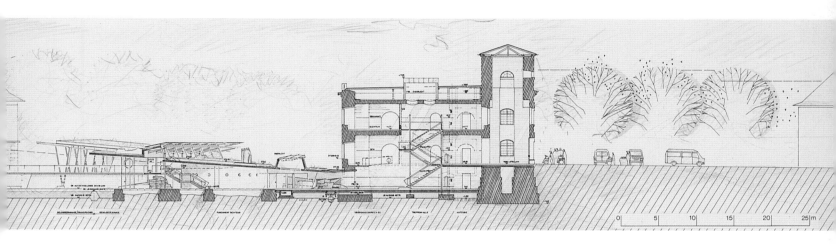

Longitudinal section, scale 1 : 500

The sports facilities are specially tailored to the educational requirements of the children, who are cared for all day long, as well as to their motor activity when making their first attempts at team games, swimming and gymnastics; they also foster the already practised skills of contact with ball, water and bicycle in a lively and secure environment. Opportunities are provided for basic experiences in contact with the great variety and depth of the construction, of its materials and hard and soft forms. The children must be able to see, touch, feel and experience the following materials and textures: cold stone, rough and smooth, warm wood, cool water, cast iron, transparent, reflecting glass, cold and warm colours.

The choice of material – concrete – and the subtly diverse ways of putting it to use have been carefully planned. With the exception of the expansive steel roof construction, all the supporting walls and roofs of the sports buildings are fashioned in smooth exposed concrete. Curved and straight wall and ceiling surfaces, sloping wall or supporting additional surfaces are formed from rough form boards. In the development hall, a section of the exposed concrete ceiling is covered over with roughcast.

Remains of the existing stonework of the former rampart site were integrated as far as possible in the interior and exterior of the architecture as a way of referring to the past and the identity of the place. Geometrically clear forms, such as cylinders and cubes, were recently added to the geometrically diffuse forms of the old fortification, and smooth, clear, exposed concrete areas were set against the irregular natural stone masonry. Whether the remains of the stonework taper off at an acute angle, or whether they still exist only in much-chiselled fragments, the new walls made from concrete appear even and sharp-edged. In addition to the tectonic structures made from concrete, steel, glass and wood, light and water determine the atmosphere of the sports buildings.

The Cavalier Elbracht is an exemplary contribution to the re-usage of buildings on former rampart sites. The enduring quality of historic structures is picked out as a central theme contributing to the building culture of the present and the past. The architecture of the sports buildings on the site of the school for the physically disabled gives an albeit individual answer to the question of what status is granted to those children who, superficially at least at first, bring less to this achievement-oriented society.

Enric Miralles

National Training Centre for Rhythmic Gymnastics
Spain – Alicante

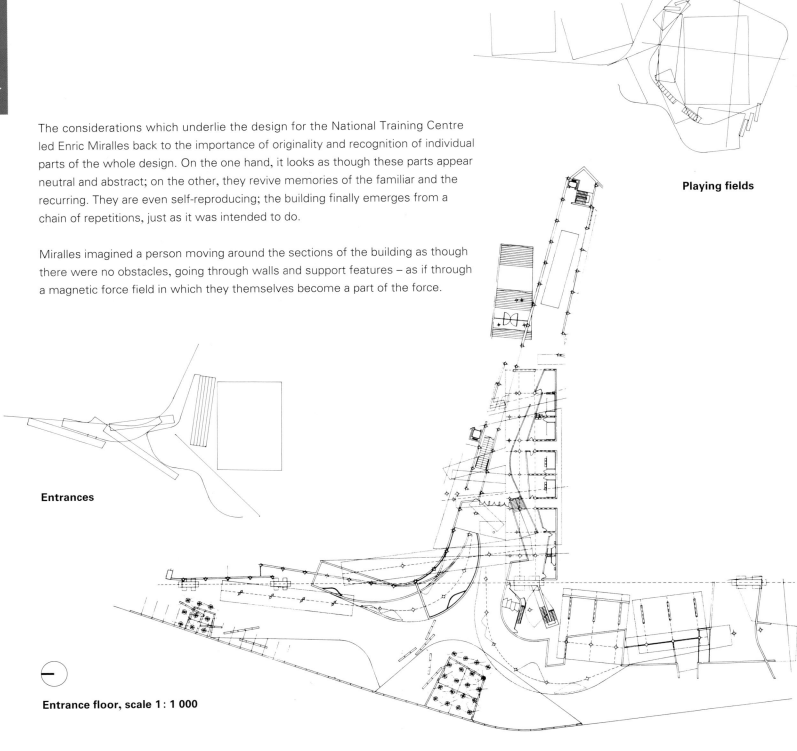

Playing fields

The considerations which underlie the design for the National Training Centre led Enric Miralles back to the importance of originality and recognition of individual parts of the whole design. On the one hand, it looks as though these parts appear neutral and abstract; on the other, they revive memories of the familiar and the recurring. They are even self-reproducing; the building finally emerges from a chain of repetitions, just as it was intended to do.

Miralles imagined a person moving around the sections of the building as though there were no obstacles, going through walls and support features – as if through a magnetic force field in which they themselves become a part of the force.

Entrances

Entrance floor, scale 1 : 1 000

If it were possible to measure the weight of the building at separate places, then the result would change constantly for Miralles, varying according to the particular location of the person in the building. Perhaps this (illusory) approach would lead to the weight of a building consisting, at certain times, of up to a third of the weight of the people using it.

The desire to use all parts of the building not only for their predetermined functions, but also to make it permanently accessible to everyone and to let them make their own decision about where they would like to situate themselves in it, is something that can already be identified in the work of the early master cathedral builders. In these historic cathedrals, there were discreet flights of narrow stairs which led into the inside of the cupola, between the outer and inner shell marking the boundary of the area, right into the top of the empty interstice. The construction of the cupola was geared to these secret ways.

Individual points of user contact within the training centre building in Alicante commissioned for the Spanish national gymnastics team –
ramps and entrance halls;
practice areas for rhythmic gymnastics;
practice areas for gymnastics;
training rooms;
facilities for dedicated players (living spaces, practice areas, showers and changing rooms,
restaurant, kitchen);
spectator stands and competition sites;
public service facilities.
All result from visibility, vista, perspective, distance and proximity.

As it caters for gymnastics and eurhythmics, those who go there to do gymnastics, as well as visitors, must enter the buildings barefoot. The perception of the material diversity – of the floor in this case – of the individual parts of the building creates a new equilibrium between human being and architecture.

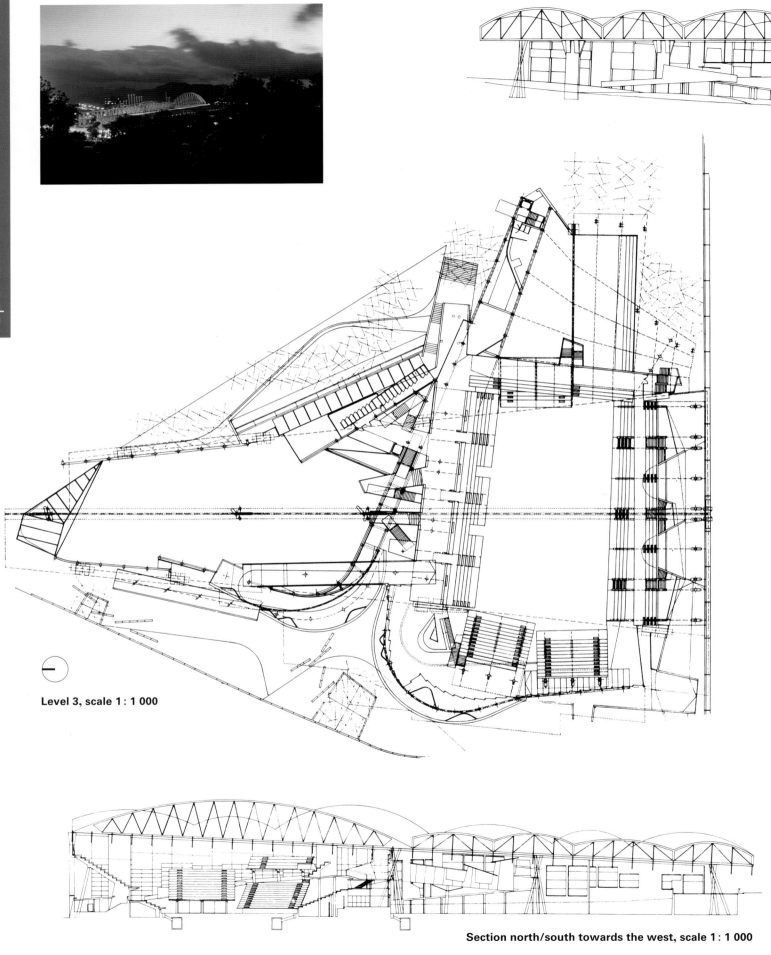

Level 3, scale 1 : 1 000

Section north/south towards the west, scale 1 : 1 000

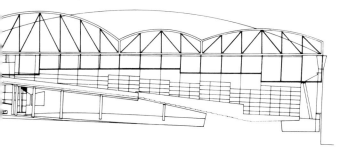

Section, scale 1 : 1 000

It seems as if the visitor, whilst walking round, could break down the entire architectural ensemble, as it were, and then reinterpret it again. The 15-metre high continuous roof unites the prefabricated parts above the sports hall with the stand for 4000 spectators and the training hall.

A series of steel box girder profiles (which visibly protrude longitudinally from the entire roof surface of the site) is constructed so that their dimensions vary depending on the load to be carried. The large arch over the sports hall can be seen from a distance.

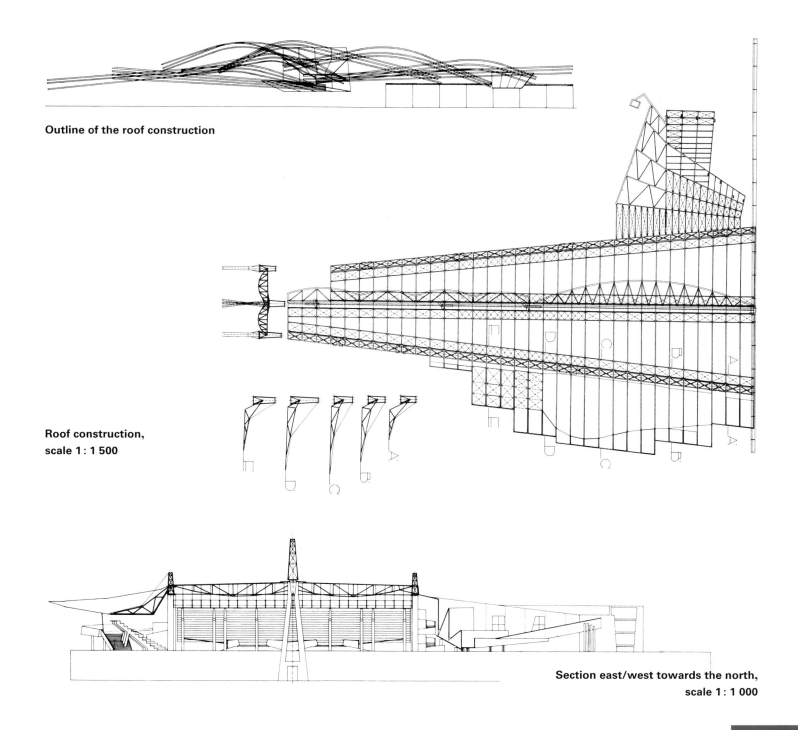

Outline of the roof construction

Roof construction, scale 1 : 1 500

Section east/west towards the north, scale 1 : 1 000

The entrance and admission areas which seem to go on forever, situated at right angles to both halls, also create a dramatic scenario – in height and profile and with cascading flights of stairs.

In order to intensify the effects of the gymnastics centre, the spectators are led onto a middle floor where they get a view of the sports area and towards the training, preparatory and rest rooms.

An excess of new, surprising, constructive prefabricated parts, striking forms which suddenly meet each other, and materials and surfaces which change quickly in detail, stands in contradiction to the carefully thought through architectural components which recur in the ground plan.

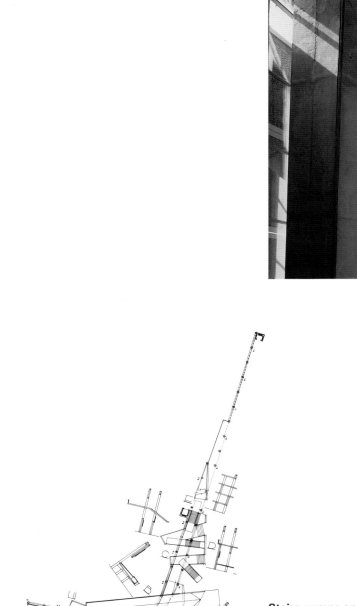

Stairs, ramps and walls of the entrance floor, scale 1 : 1 500

The strong desire of Enric Miralles to attain a spontaneous effect on the player as on each individual visitor of the gymnastics centre is realised in the direct contact between the individual and the building. This piece of architecture is best described as a 'piece of architecture for movement' – for players and spectators alike.

Patrick Berger

'Dojo régional' Judo Hall
France – Brétigny-sur-Orge near Paris

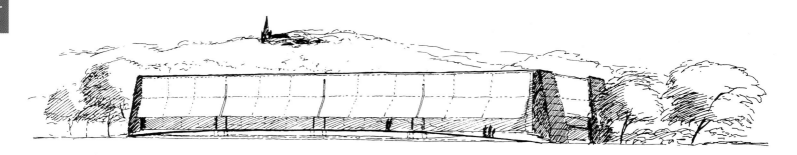

For Patrick Berger, architecture is the recollection of what is essential – composition and density, untouched material, and their application to construction and form. Adolf Loos let himself be impressed by a simple, sharp-edged formed stone found by the wayside while travelling through Nepal – to him, this was proof of both simplicity and cosmos. For Patrick Berger, the ideal of the original exists when he fathoms the future ('L'origine est devant nous' – 'The beginning is ahead of us') in his architectural language which has a Zen-Buddhist effect.

On the southern access road to Brétigny-sur-Orge, near Paris, the Dojo rises up self-importantly in the midst of yet another purposelessly developed built-up area situated on the outskirts. Nothing more than a strong, closed corpus made from wood, highly chiselled, and tied to four strong reinforced concrete towers, the Dojo can be seen from a distance.

Resistant to all tendencies towards dispersal or fragmentation, the construction hovers as a horizontal block, three metres high. The volume, 66 metres in length, also denies the architectural play of openings. Neither symbol nor contemporary document, the Dojo seems transported through time as if it were holding shadow rather than light in its interior.

What stand out are the particular development of the entrance floors, the formal distance and use, which have been reconciled.

View of the western side

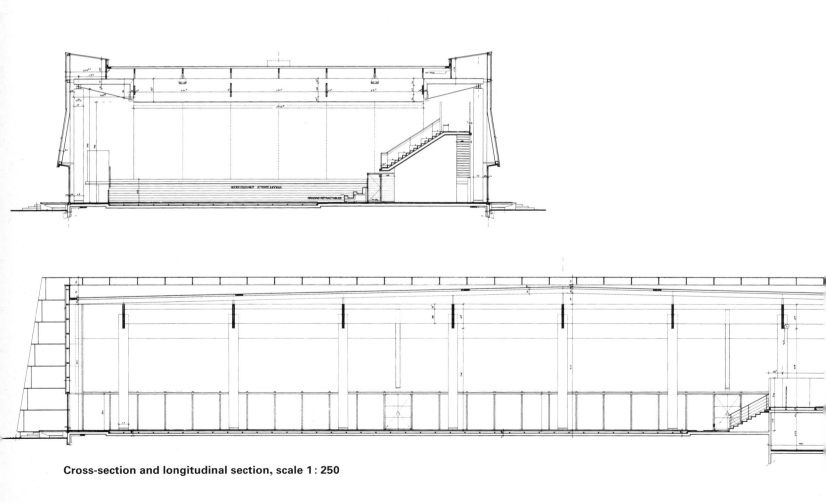

Cross-section and longitudinal section, scale 1 : 250

Surrounded by the remains of a stream, the wooden ground platform rises five steps high and appears to be suspended over the gravel field. Inside, all areas of the large hall are covered with wall-to-wall carpets in order to create an ideal environment for the martial art of judo. Finally, the glass façades enclose the building in a precise geometry. These are only interrupted where entrances draw attention to themselves as closed wooden panels.

In a large hall-like room for the Japanese sport of judo, Patrick Berger connects the sports area to stands for over 600 spectators and a gently raised training area. The facilities are located underneath.

The atmosphere of the hall is determined by sparse constructional elements, by the smooth-surfaced, panelled wooden walls of the corpus, and by a fanlight on one of the longitudinal sides.

Regularity, repetition and symmetry are methods which are employed economically, intensified by the sparseness of the materials which have been left in their natural state. Without showing off or arousing contradiction, Patrick Berger introduces us to a special piece of architecture characterised by poetic stillness and the unity of shadow and light.

South façade, interior

Massimiliano Fuksas

Sports Hall and Playing Field in the Candie-Saint-Bernard Block of Flats
France – Paris

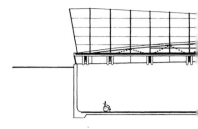

Faubourg Saint-Antoine near the Bastille is seen as one of the districts in Paris whose fragile, urbane network has regained sufficient charisma to attract new inhabitants. Fuksas took on an urban developmental strategy, the aim of which is to safeguard the regeneration of the city, its great variety of human circumstances and the preservation of its architectural heritage by means of careful structural interventions. The social structure of Faubourg Saint-Antoine with its compact blocks of houses interrupted by a large number of passages, is an urbane mix of workshops, tenement houses, trend-conscious fashion shops and lots of small and larger restaurants.

Site plan – sports building in the urban estate, scale 1: 2 000

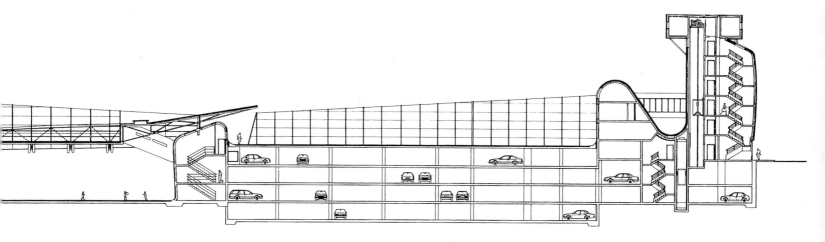

This part of town consists of a multitude of sites, either vacant or lying unused, which Fuksas defines as empty spaces, as 'hollowed out notches'. He was less concerned with arranging architectural completion than detecting the partly invisible energy which this district needs for living and for its diverse activities. This bewitching disorder full of subtle order in the Faubourg Saint-Antoine can be discovered everywhere if – like Fuksas – you search behind the street façades, and go beyond the usual images.

The job of implementing a compact, structural intervention on the expansive building plot could quickly become too much for the features of the city environment. Fuksas therefore decided not to build over part of the site so that constant urban change could continue to be a feature of the district.

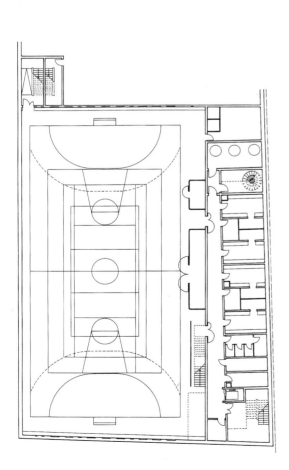

Scale 1 : 500

The core design concept is implemented with a wave-like residential development which flows down to the ground on the Rue de Candie. The wave forms a valley to the courtyard side, rises again – in a smaller wave movement – and gives way to a playing field under which an underground car park is built over four floors. The wave peters out to the Rue de Candie with a sports hall embedded underground and a tennis court situated on the roof of the hall.

The ceiling of the buried sports hall is raised unspectacularly. Light penetrates the hall sufficiently from the sides and also from the street. For the passers-by on the Rue de Candie, the diverse life of the district is reflected in the windows of the sports hall. The roof structure with steel braces and sectional girders which work like scaffolding, filters the light.

Towards Rue Charles Delescluze

Towards Rue de Candie

Flats on Rue Charles Delescluze

Barriers, similar to those found on a building site, protect the tennis court on the roof from the bustling city – or do the filters offer protection from the tennis court? In the Parisian suburb of the Faubourg Saint-Antoine, the city is always full of vitality as it is, even in the courtyard of the street.

Between the sports hall and the multi-storey car park, or between the two playing fields, a connecting street, similar to a passage, cuts across the site. From here, there are entrances to the underground car park, the underground changing rooms, and the cafeteria.

Fuksas sees the north–south superstructure between Rue Charles Delescluze and Rue de Candie as an urban developmental concept of transition and of the unfinished. The visible dynamism and perceptible tension are derived from the relationship of building and emptiness – from a dynamic concept which architecture does not convey, but which it can nevertheless summon.

Alain Pélissier

Gymnase du Lycée Gustave Eiffel
France – Talange

Sports halls usually have a dubious, whitish-yellow resonance for most people, probably because that's what almost all their personal experiences tell them. For one person, the steamy atmosphere of badly ventilated changing rooms is a total turn-off, for the less sporty, the 'gymnasium' is a large torture chamber – and even those who have achieved sweat-inducing performance records share these unpleasant memories.

But nowadays 'physical training' has been replaced by the physique-focused 'body-styling' which has already been introduced in schools. But is architecture also pursuing a new identity, one that can maintain its hold on the market and in a structual context?

Alain Pélissier has situated his astonishingly economical metal building on a small flood-protected hill meadow. When visiting the simple sports hall, the brightness of the open hall stands out, and this first impression sticks. It is clear that 'transparency' has had a determining influence on the design – in both directions. Under an obligation to the man who gave his name to the Lycée, Gustave Eiffel, and in homage to the historic past of the metal-processing industry in the region, the small building teaches metal construction.

Rigorous economising is also very much in evidence, after the town did not – as planned – contribute to the costs. The simplicity called for led to the design being realised as a low-budget pure metal construction, 'à petit pris', free from any non-functional frills, on a 'what you see is what you get' basis. Three sides and the roof area are closed, the northern side is transparent – architecture can be this practical. The combination of material and form is just as convincing. Four slim porticos made from extremely thin, measured, curved, tubular steel support tapering, half-timbered lattice girders on which the ultra-light, metal sandwich roof is suspended: a delicately slender and web-like power play of load, load shedding and load direction change.

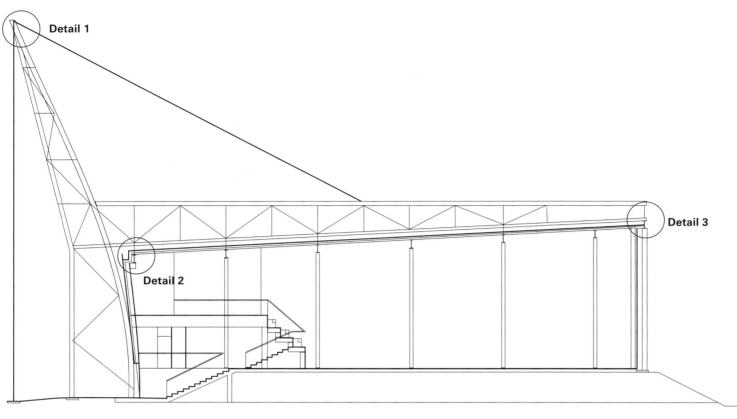

Detail 1

Detail 2

Detail 3

Section of construction,
scale 1 : 250

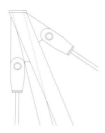

Detail 1

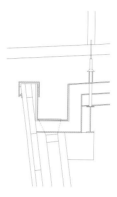

Detail 2

Detail 3

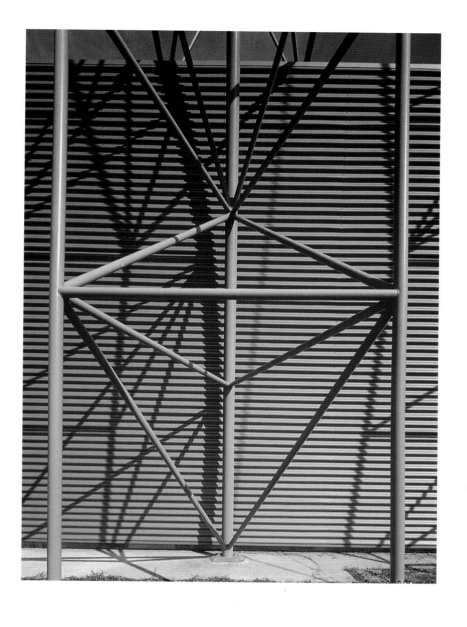

The northern glass and steel façade is suspended as a curtain wall and this slims down the V-shaped supporting structure. The three closed metal walls made of the sandwich panels, horizontally corrugated on the outside, encase the square hall which has a floor area of 33 x 33 metres.

There is no architecture or symbolism anywhere here. Instead, everywhere you look, you see 'practical' solutions in terms of material, form and structure. The conceptual contribution consists of reduction and concentration, a possibly calculated expression of the – as requested – economical, low budget, ecological and functional construction. The pleasantly modest Alain Pélissier has succeeded in becoming a forward-looking 'icon' of the modern age, timeless and ever-significant.

Toyo Ito

Baseball Hall: O-Shaped Dome
Japan – Odate

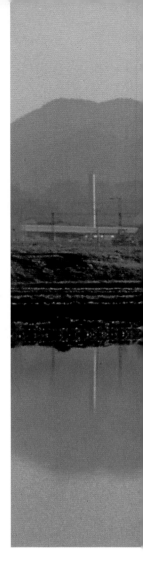

The 1964 Olympic Games in Tokyo marked a new era in Japan: with the introduction of a computer-controlled reservation system for the high-speed tram, the Shinkansen, in the Olympic year of the mechanical-industrial age, Japan catapulted itself straight into the electronic age.

For Toyo Ito, the architecture of the new, electronic era is able to reorient itself, free of the icons of the mechanical age – aeroplanes, cars, ships, machinery: what is important now are the flow of energy and information, the interaction of different technology systems (layers), or new worlds of form and information, right up to the bar code.

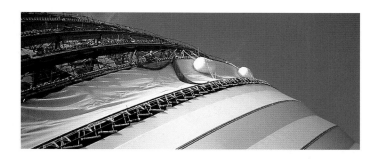

With the baseball hall in Odate, Toyo Ito realises the encounter with the changing times, announced programmatically by his 'LITE Architecture'. The aim: to build in a weightlessly transparent style and for a limited lifespan, a construction influenced by abstraction, possessing an expressive form and a geometric rigidity. The baseball hall in Odate appears suspended and incorporeal in its construction. The effect of the expanse as well as that of the light is to activate an intense, almost artificial atmosphere.

The concept of the hall shows a slightly eccentric, semicircular form. Without integration into an urban context, this presents itself as autonomous and unconnected. The presence of a dematerialised construction and of its folded, transparent surface permits connections with media, information and information carriers which make the invisible visible with just a tiny microchip.

As if it were a set of building blocks, the wooden structure appears to be broken down into wooden beam sections which are then fixed to wide arches. Filigree wooden/tubular steel half-timbering penetrates the arches of the beam sections in a transverse direction. In order to achieve a suspended effect, the superstructure begins on a ring of reinforced concrete which is held upright symmetrically with supports placed at an angle. The surface of the superstructure, which is made from two translucent, clam-shell, Teflon™ membranes, is wired so that it forms folds.

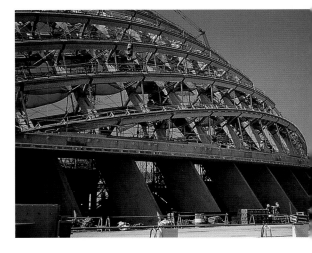

A form emerges which is reminiscent of the mathematical form of a Chinese lantern, of the constructive form of an object of the universe, or which looks back to the aesthetics of origami. The aesthetic effect of the folded surface, and the simple geometry in outline and section raise the boundary between abstract study and playful realisation. The dimensions of the hall are as follows: 175 metres long, 157 metres wide and 42 metres high. The building seems to consist of an expressively constructed surface structure alone. This character is reinforced by the modulation of light and reflection towards constantly changing information.

Toyo Ito has succeeded in entering the electronic age with his baseball hall design. The lightness and transparency of the hall are presented to visitors and sports enthusiasts as a minimalistic, ecological formula, as the combination of reduction of material and economy of weight.

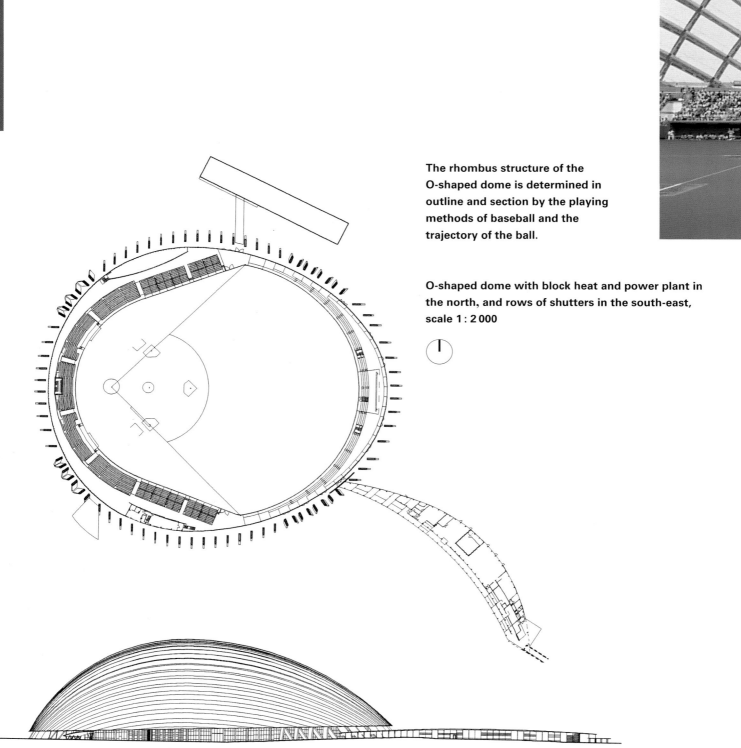

The rhombus structure of the O-shaped dome is determined in outline and section by the playing methods of baseball and the trajectory of the ball.

O-shaped dome with block heat and power plant in the north, and rows of shutters in the south-east, scale 1 : 2 000

Peter Stürzebecher

Columbia Swimming Pool
Germany – Berlin

An open-air swimming pool had once stood on this site. That was in 1952 when the first open-air swimming pools in these districts were built in accordance with an 'emergency programme' for the areas of West Berlin, Neuköllen and Wedding, which, at that time, had the highest population densities. It is difficult to fathom now why the district of Neuköllen planned their pool to sit directly next to Tempelhof Airport and on an expressway.

Many people have one lasting memory of this: how a terrain was modelled out of the rubble, and how even council employees worked on it after hours and at weekends in order to make sure that a 'summer pool' would be built in record time.

When, 35 years later, the pool became derelict through erosion and corrosion, they made the pragmatic decision to demolish it, and set up a competition to choose the most suitable architect for a new building. The existing pools, terraces and pergolas were features worth maintaining.

The design can be interpreted as a dialogue with Kandinsky's artistic age, or as a reference to the original 1950s' pool on this site – or even as an expression of our (philosophically viewed) present, 'multi-polar' time which has characterised the concept of architecture and the scenic layout. What is clear is that Berlin, after the fall of the Wall, wanted and supported construction on this spot which met aesthetic requirements, opened out towards the city, and which would have a large city clientele.

A two-winged main building accommodating changing rooms and shower/toilet facilities, and a café-restaurant on two levels now replace the previous buildings. With a new paddling pool for children, the pool attendant's area and the 'toboggan'(a large water slide), the site today meets the standards of an architecturally disciplined 'adventure pool' situated in the open air, built with steel, wood and glass, and moulded by the surrounding scenery.

Quality carries a price – and yet, it does not have to be expensive. The architecture and frugal space allocation make it possible to fulfil the goal of economy: cost-saving construction. In addition, the block heat and power plant saves on energy.

Main building with changing rooms and shower/toilet facilities

Site plan:
Main building
Café-restaurant
Pool attendant's house
Toboggan
Block heat and power plant
WC area
Swimming pools
Depot area with entrance wall

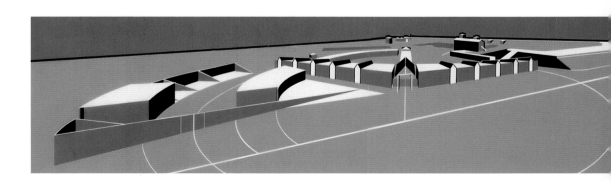

In the middle of the site is the 'toboggan', a winding slide, 100 metres long, which was tested first of all in model experiments. But where is the public to stand, while they wait to slide down the chute? In order to avoid queues restricting access to the pool, or moving precariously up a spiral staircase, those waiting are instead raised up onto a higher level. The 'admissions building' has turned into the path which, in the guise of a wooden footbridge going through two wooden platform houses, leads straight through to the 10 metre high 'launch pad', from where sliding and surfing can begin.

What is going on in the pool can be easily observed from the two floors of the restaurant and café terraces. Two curved flights of stairs made from steel – regarded as sculptures in the landscape – lead onto the glass veranda of the long, filigree building. With the ample terraces which are situated in front of it, the restaurant building makes an ideal playground.

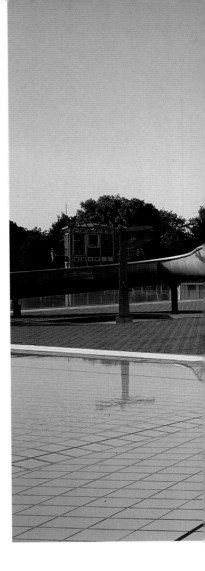

Café-restaurant, sunbathing area

Toboggan

Paddling pool

The small, solitary buildings of the pool attendant's cabin and the WC facilities are a variation on the typical design of a house with clear, cubist structures, a pavilion roof, blue wooden surfaces, and carefully fashioned details. The precision work and colour studies of these prototypes were also used for the main building's changing rooms, showers and toilets.

Squared off and stretched out and accompanied by an avenue of trees, the main building plants an urban developmental signal for a structurally controlled piece of architecture in steel and wood along the Columbia embankment. The rich blue colour of the outer wall forms a contrast to the light furnishings in the interior of the building. The main building, surrounding scenery and swimming pool area can be seen through glass slits which are positioned at the same height as the building.

The Columbia baths are more than a swimming pool, though: a city depot area with offices, storage space, factory yard and car parks, is integrated behind a continuous, seemingly infinitely long entrance wall positioned on an incline.

The architectural housing appears concrete, creative and also inviting from the outside. The 'Columbia' provides a topic for communication for observers who drive past quickly as well as for the visitors who use the pool. And for the multitude of visitors – up to 15 000 on a hot summer's day – it has a relaxing effect. A happy atmosphere prevails.

Upper level of the café-restaurant

View of the street from the Columbia embankment, main building and entrance

Swimming pool attendant's cabin

The country park – as if it were a solitary patch of grassland – compliments the architecture. The valuable stock of trees was preserved. Connections between the separate buildings are structurally emphasised by entwining pergolas, shaped in flowing lines of arches supposedly reminiscent of the vibrant forms of the original baths of the 1950s. With paths, cobbled and fashioned areas, with areas for sunbathing, benches and small decorative items, an environmentally oriented atmosphere is conveyed. The choice of renewable building material, wood, in its fundamental significance for storage of CO_2, is an ecological marker and an environmentally-friendly component of the entire site.

Realistic and sensory architecture and sports-related leisure time, art and ecology, fun by the pool and the countryside experience are all interlinked in the 'Columbia'. The site was awarded the Holzbau prize in 1996, and the IOC/IAKS award in 1997 of the Association for Sports and Leisure Facilities of the International Olympic Committee.

Aside from the modern mix of architectural excellence and sophisticated staging at the 'Columbia', there is still a whiff of the aura of Georges Seurat's Impressionist masterpiece, *Bathers at Asnières*, painted in 1884 – almost a century before this building. It shows men and youths under the hot sun and in glistening colours who stand in the water limply and with expressionless faces, or hang about on the strand. Items of clothing lie scattered on the grass and, in the distance, clouds of smoke billow from factory chimneys and trains.

In Berlin, it is the Tempelhof Airport which borders the grounds of the 'Columbia'. From here, aeroplanes full of modern sports nomads who indulge in the ideal image of slim youthfulness, take off into the distance for exotic water paradises.

Luis Moreno Mansilla and Emilio Tunón

San Fernando de Henares Swimming Centre
Spain – Madrid

In the middle of the 19th century in Europe, they started building public baths for personal hygiene for the benefit of the city inhabitants. After the end of the First World War in the 1920s, the first swimming centres were built within the framework of a style of town planning which was shaped by the modern age. In new districts and estates, swimming centres (open all year round) or summer baths were structurally combined with schools and playing fields. The swimming centre in San Fernando de Henares, an industrial suburb of Madrid, corresponds to this typical pattern. An older summer bath, a sports hall, and a stadium nearby, together with the swimming centre of Mansilla and Tunón, form a loose ensemble of sports buildings.

Entrance side, south-west

The architecture of the San Fernando swimming centre is loaded with diverse themes.

The functional and architectural division between inside and outside is achieved according to the house-within-a-house principle. An outer cover of narrow, concrete lamellae, layered one on top of the other, encloses the inner glass cover like a grid. The lamellae are openly stacked on top of each other so that the hall is exposed in a particular way: a filter effect of light emerges. The roof of the swimming centre is covered.

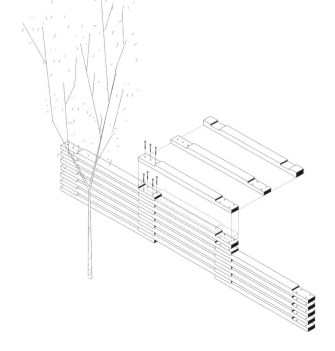

Interlaced effect on the façade

Light penetrates the outer cover into the interior of the swimming centre (70 x 22 metres). The filtered light from the outside creates graphic patterns on the exercise areas around the pool. This stimulates associations with the worlds of film and of computers.

Light is either absorbed by or reflected on the surface of the water. Moreover, the latter appears to be sinking. The swimmer experiences this play of light when surfacing. The movement of water caused by the swimmer produces countless optical reflexes. As with the images of a kaleidoscope, the interplay of water and light produces a dreamlike atmosphere.

David Hockney, one of the key figures in the London pop scene of the 1960s, impressed Mansilla and Tunón with his artistic studies of the architectural dimension of water and light. Through Hockney, they studied his varied observations that depended on the different effects of daylight, time and brightness. Refraction and reflection of light, transparency, and shimmering change which occur when a swimmer moves in the water were documented in 1978, in a series of 29 'Piscines de papier' ('paper swimming pools'). Water in the architectural sphere and the presence of the person in water are Mansilla and Tunón's conceptual starting points for the swimming centre in San Fernando de Henares.

The architects are not so much concerned with the atmosphere; light and water in the architectural sphere are the focus of Mansilla and Tunón. They want to control the natural power of the light just like photographers and make it subject to the architecture. The light does not pervade the swimming centre in currents, but rather as a fine, sharply cut web of thin, interrupted and converging lines.

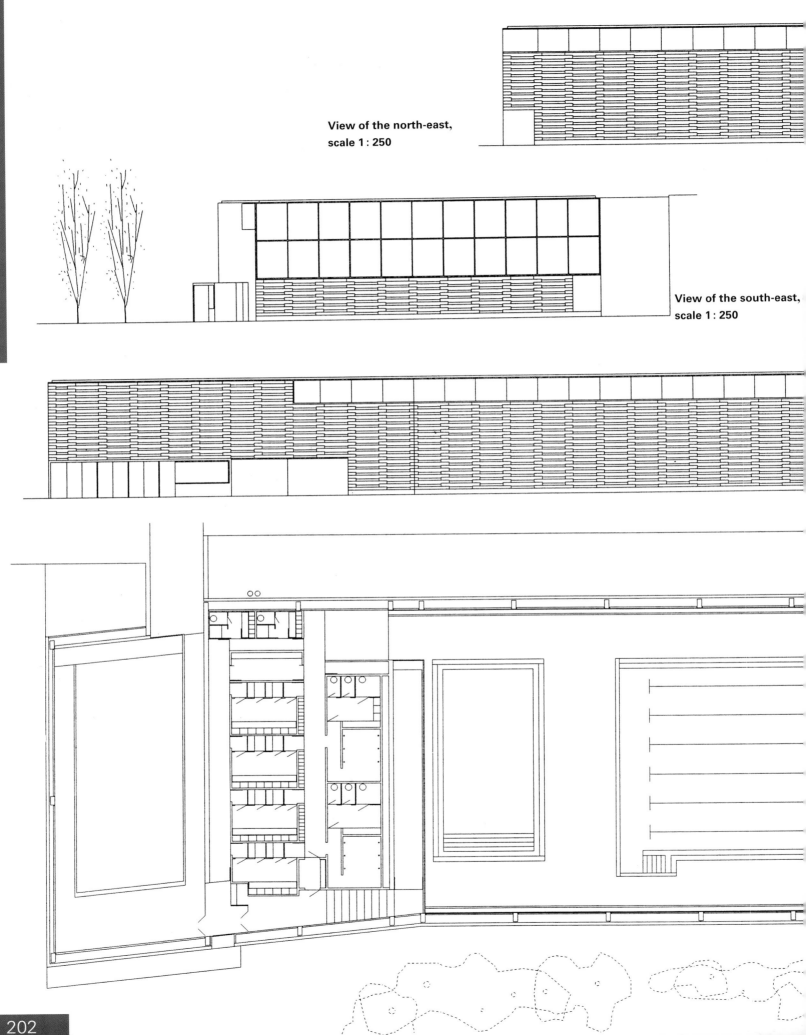

View of the north-east,
scale 1 : 250

View of the south-east,
scale 1 : 250

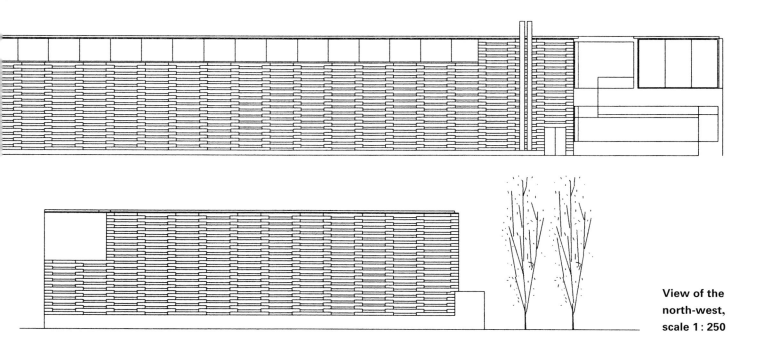

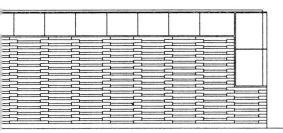

View of the
north-west,
scale 1 : 250

View of the south-west, entrance side,
scale 1 : 250

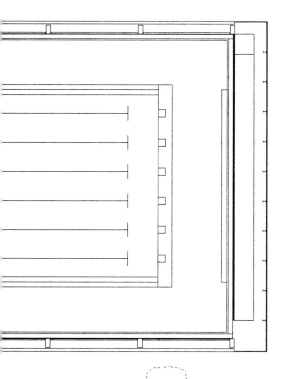

Ground plan, scale 1 : 250

The building concept is uncompromising: as a pure cube, the swimming centre is positioned one level above the site. Below it, level with the ground, are the technical facilities. It is not possible to build a cellar because of the high level of ground water. A linear sequence of functions – entrance hall as a divider with a ramp to the upper level, changing rooms, teaching pool and multi-purpose pool – supports this clear concept. The entrance hall positioned at the height of the building connects both floors via a ramp which runs along the side of the walls.

Pictures such as Pierre Bonnard's *Bathers* from 1925 anticipate impressively the atmosphere of Mansilla and Tunón's swimming centre.

Tadao Ando

Swimming Pool in a Shopping Centre
Japan – Tokyo

On the most important shopping street in Minami Aoyama, a fashionable residential area in Tokyo, is land for building – there, where the buildings appear non-uniform and hopelessly disintegrated.

The commercial premises, 'Collezione' by Tadao Ando, with boutiques, apartments and the 'Holonix' sports centre with swimming pool and sports hall, seek to mediate between the cultural continuity of Japanese architecture and the processes that endanger it, triggered by progress and civilisation.

The city dwellers of the 21st century believe that the sports centre should be open to all social classes and age groups. One of the aims of the 'Holonix' is to help everyone fulfil their individual sporting interests in perfect harmony.

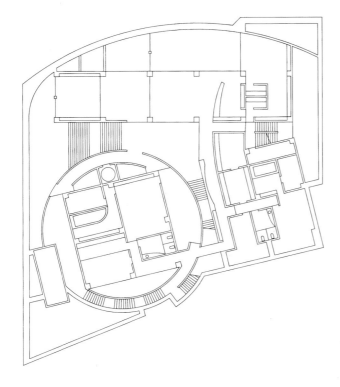

First basement level, scale 1 : 500

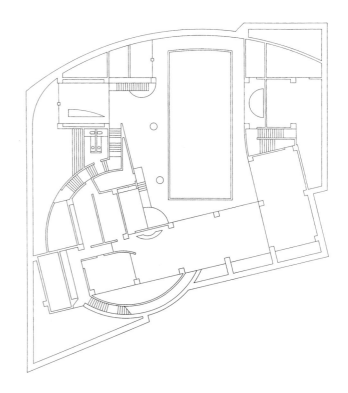

Second basement level, scale 1 : 500

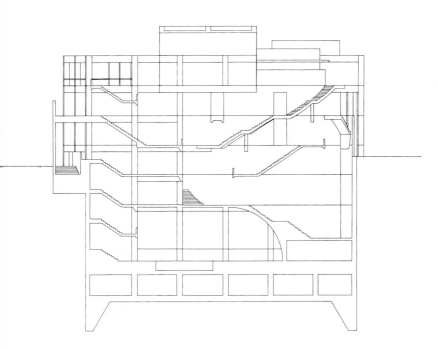

Section, scale 1 : 500

Simple geometric principles of order help to set the building into its chaotic surroundings. Tadao Ando's intention is to take up the hopeless struggle with the urbane reality of Tokyo and yet accept inevitable defeat.

The inclusion of natural conditions on all levels of the building even into the three underground storeys emphasises the intention to create distance from the destructive logic of the city of Tokyo.

In order to follow the lines of the surrounding buildings, Tadao Ando covers the plot of land for building with two right-angled grid spans rotated at an angle of 13.5 degrees from which rise up right-angled, three-dimensional forms built from reinforced concrete.

The aim of these is to produce the horizontal connection with the city and surrounding buildings. A cube acts as a mediator between the forms. A cylindrical volume connects the three basement levels vertically with the four upper floors of the premises. Light comes in through the cylinder, and links the poles of sky and earth. Nature gains admittance.

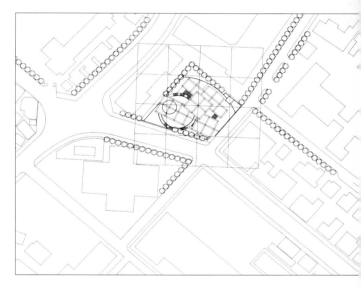

Site plan, scale 1 : 2 500

Entrance to the subterranean swimming centre, which is twice as high as one of the storeys and has a pool 20 x 12.5 metres large, is inconspicuous. The path passes through the building diagonally, and through widening stairs, leads to a room whose rays of light are refracted off the simple walls made of reinforced concrete: simple communication.

In comparison with Western architecture, the appointed interpretative resources have a simplifying effect in order to impress on the visitor shape and material, light and nature, (site) engineering and tradition, or even poetry and utility.

Without producing a glistening effect, light penetrates the centre from the cylinder in a razor-sharp and contrasting way. Shaded areas, created by indirect light coming in, have a more subdued effect. We can perhaps find traces here of a connection to Tadao Ando's favourite works by Piranesi, *Carceri*, and even more so to *Chiaroscuri*.

Comparable to a 'parcours architectural', the swimming centre is diagonally opened up 12 metres deep into the second basement floor with narrow passageways and stairs which fan out. The prevailing feeling here is of peace and quiet and detachment from the noise of Tokyo. Attached to the swimming centre are a sauna, beauty salon, massage and make-up studios as well as changing and shower rooms, a training room, club rooms and a restaurant. The upper floors of the shopping centre are accessible via a spiral staircase located on the outer side of the cylinder. Customers get to individual shops from here.

The vertical, empty space between the cuboid and cylindrical volumes – from the lowest basement floor to the highest storey – is terraced and landscaped like a waterfall. Unobstructed views, reflections or shadows intensify the visitors' feeling for light and wind, for the unity of nature and architectural space, as they make their way through the building.

Paavo Karjaleinen and Arktes Oy

Adventure Pool in a Hotel
Finland – Oulu

Oulu, Finland, is situated 200 kilometres below the polar circle on the Baltic Sea. The sea here is frozen over for four to five months of the year and summers are short. Swimming in the open air is possible for only four to six weeks in the summer. With 150 000 inhabitants, the town would not have been able to finance its own swimming pool. The Eden Hotel with its spa and artificial subtropical area for recuperation at a pleasant temperature and with modern equipment for individual body toning – offered the solution for Oulu.

The concept of the hotel complex with its 100 beds, conference rooms, auditorium for an audience of 140, a restaurant with seating for 700, together with an adventure pool with treatment, fitness and beauty facilities, all fitted into an area of 2200 square metres, is adapted so that it can stay open all year round. The siting of the architectural space promotes an international ambience. For 'recreational nomads' and globe-trotters with a sporting bent, Hotel Eden is a favoured location. Within the space of a few years, two million visitors and guests have enjoyed the hotel and its facilities.

Initial considerations at the planning stage were the proximity of the building, restaurant and open terraces to the beach, the view of the sea from the adventure pool, and usage of natural daylight as well as an energy-saving design.

The epicentre of the site is located four metres above beach level: this is the artificial subtropical room covered by a glass dome. Changing rooms, showers and toilets are located in the basement. The sun terraces and restaurant are situated peripherally in a perfect circle around the pool, and in line with the sea.

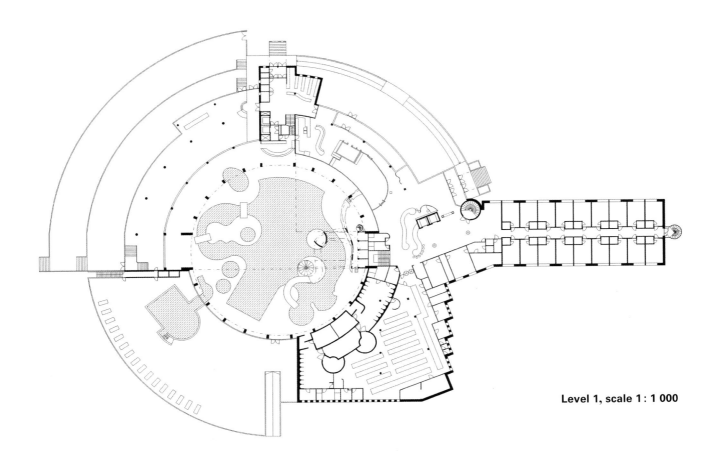

Level 1, scale 1 : 1 000

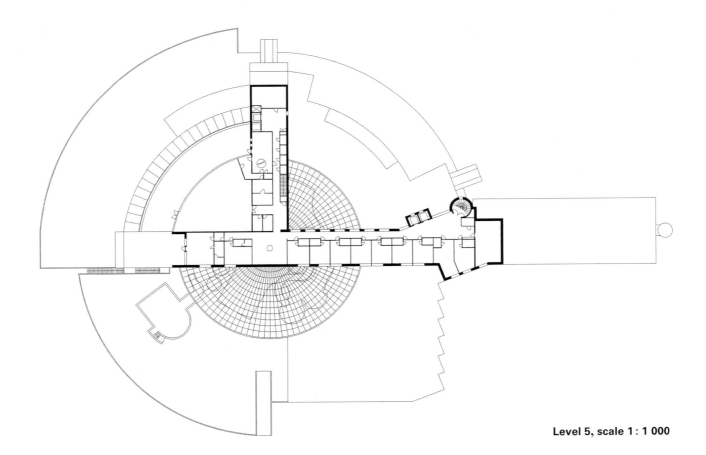

Level 5, scale 1 : 1 000

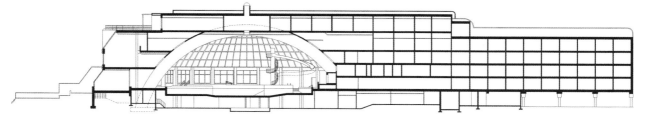

Section, scale 1 : 1 000

The differences in temperature ranging from –35 degrees Celsius in the winter to +30 degrees in the summer, and the variations in exposure to sunlight – from three hours' daylight in winter up to 24 hours in the summer – determine the requirements for the construction, vegetation and energy concept. Surrounded by subtropical plants, visitors are meant to feel as though they are in the open air.

The constant atmospheric humidity of 55 per cent, room temperature of 32 degrees, and (energy-saving) water temperature of 30 degrees guarantee a clear view of the sea, even in extreme weather conditions. The double glazing of the glass dome with its aluminium supports, and an additional layer of circulating air prevent ice from forming on the exterior. Solar radiation provides a surplus of heat from as early as March.

The internal climatic corresponds to the growth cycle of the subtropical vegetation. There is a lack of natural daylight in January and February; but the summer makes up for it with almost 24 hours of daylight.

Paavo Karjalainen, architect of Arktes Oy, describes his own experience of a winter night in the subtropical pool at the Hotel Eden: '... the temperature was –10 degrees and all around snow lay over the frozen Baltic Sea. I was swimming, relaxed, in the outer pool with friends when, in the starlit night sky – something that can only be experienced near the polar circle – I suddenly saw a lunar eclipse, completely unexpectedly.'

David Chipperfield

River and Rowing Museum
Great Britain – Henley-on-Thames

In an age when globalisation has reached even architecture, concentration on the essential and the integral requires a bold aloofness – in a timeless spirit.

For a select group of architects, placing the traces of the place, the history and the materials to the fore equates with a silent appreciation of beauty and well-being among the generally banal. This group includes David Chipperfield, Alvaro Siza, José Rafael Moneo, Tadao Ando, Luis Barragán and Carlo Scarpa.

The sensuality of the material and of the natural variation in light creates shape, volume and space. The limited number of architectural interventions paves the way for the indspensable: space, light and material.

This basic approach may conceal an excess of practicality. For David Chipperfield, 'theoretical practice' and 'practical theory' are one and the same. Gilles Deleuze adds: 'Strictly speaking, a theory is a tool box. It has nothing to do with its initiator. It has to be useful. It has to work, but not by itself.'

Henley-on-Thames, an hour's drive to the west of London, has been the venue for the traditional regatta every year since 1851. From its beginnings as a small holiday resort for spectators and boats, the construction of a small museum lent it the impetus to go beyond its makeshift status. The museum, which boasted a collection of historic rowing boats, a history of rowing and of the town itself, was designed to reflect the conservative spirit of Henley.

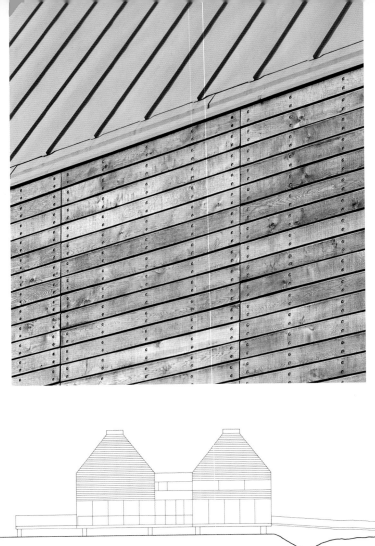

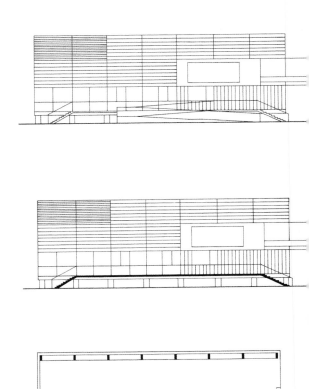

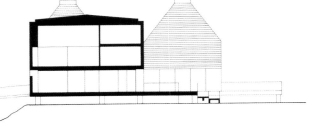

Picture gallery, boat collection, scale 1 : 500

The glass base with restaurant, library, sales and service facilities, storage,
scale 1 : 500

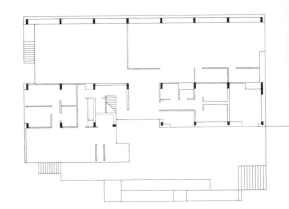

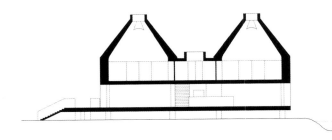

Scale 1 : 500

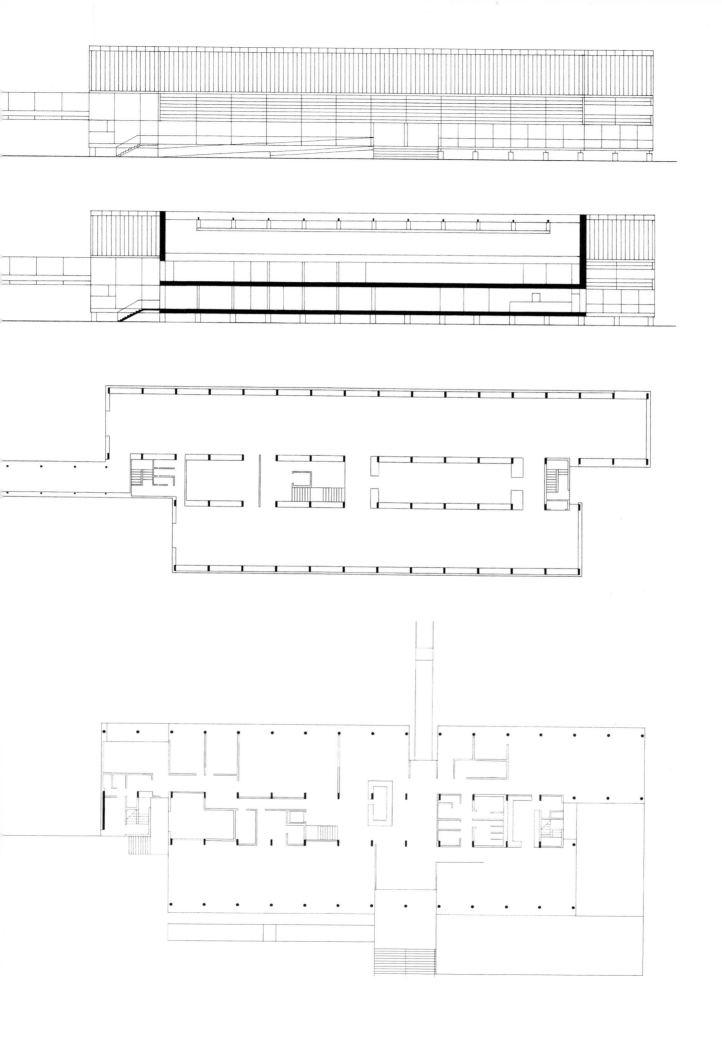

The scenic landscape, traditional boating houses on the banks of the Thames and the shape of the boats, are reproduced in simplified form in the two long houses, and appear to swim like capsized ships over a glass base in the waters of the Thames.

The wooden barns and boathouses along the Thames are picked out as a central theme, adding shape, material and detail to a new composition. The two long houses are locked to the walls with a flat wooden board.

The saddleback roofs are encased in zinc plate. Slits of light along the ridges shine down. There are rooms of silence, seclusion, and a concentration on the boat collection and picture gallery. In contrast, the glass-enveloped basement rooms open out on all sides.

The glass base also appears to float. Similar to a Japanese temple, the base plate of the glass volume is held by a few solid concrete supports, connected to the ground via stairways and ramps. The basement with the restaurant, library, shop, service and administration rooms, and museum storage reflects the surrounding river and meadow landscape – enhanced by unframed, membrane-like glass surfaces.

Victor Mani

Netherlands Sports Museum
The Netherlands – Lelystad

An impossible task. At a time when top class sport, advertising and the sale of sports goods reached dizzy heights, a sports museum with an unprecedentedly low budget was to be built in Lelystadt. Inspired by this challenge, an imaginative, unconventional project was developed, pure in both overview and detail: 'Where there is nothing, everything is possible,' claimed Rem Koolhaas as early as 1985.

A private trust enabled a museum to be built, housing a permanent collection and varying exhibitions. The fact that the new museum was opened in May 1995 by Prince Willem Alexander after just one year's construction shows respect for the great accomplishment of Victor Mani. The prince, a sporting hero, regularly participates successfully in the 197.5 kilometre long Eleven Towns race, the Dutch national skating event.

South façade in wood and glass with anti-glare polyester sheets

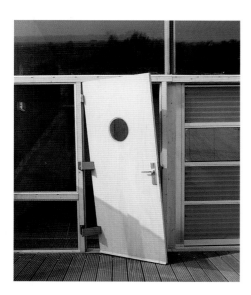

After overcoming a series of financial setbacks, the first phase of construction was completed: a large public exhibition space with a ticket counter, adjoining rooms and a coffee bar. Once the next construction phase became financially viable, further exhibition spaces and a large sports hall would be built.

The entire museum is still not fully complete, but the architectural hallmark is already clearly recognisable: a long, attenuated building, two floors – like an upturned reinforced concrete table – and a lightweight steel roof construction. The two floors are connected via a ramp and staircase. This develops into a fascinating plinth landscape of sloping layers and bevels. From the exterior, the dyke ridge penetrates the building, a reminder that Lelystad was created from the sea. The spacious setting of sculpturally inserted elements, which gives rise to an exciting landscape for exhibitions at entry level, could also be used as a grandstand for the future sports hall.

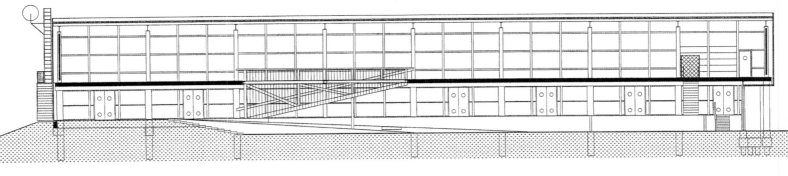

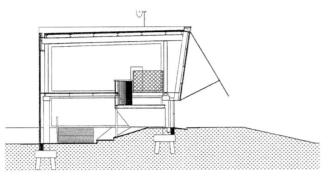

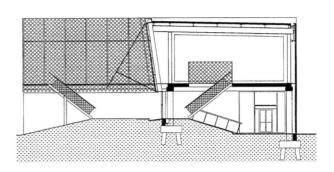

Various sections, scale 1 : 300

A successful atmosphere of industrial design has developed. The corrugated floor is geometrically arranged in a 50-50 grid to form a simple concrete footpath. Victor Mani avoids the need for elaborate sealing solutions for the long south façade thanks to their slanted position, which protects against the weather. The low-cost, transparent, corrugated polyester sheets form a cost- and energy-effective façade on this side over the height of two floors. To be more precise: a 100 per cent double façade in the upper level, a 50 per cent double façade in the middle level, and a single façade in the bottom level. The result is a 50 per cent saving in energy. The anti-glare effect is a stroke of genius: the protective plate fins used in agriculture, mounted with fixings used in shipbuilding, reduce construction costs considerably.

The success story of Charles Eames, who innovatively developed elegant, poetic and comfortable furniture, structural components and houses using industrial parts and simple technologies, was pursued by Victor Mani in the first construction phase of the sports museum. And still the story continues to unfold...

View of the southern side, entrances

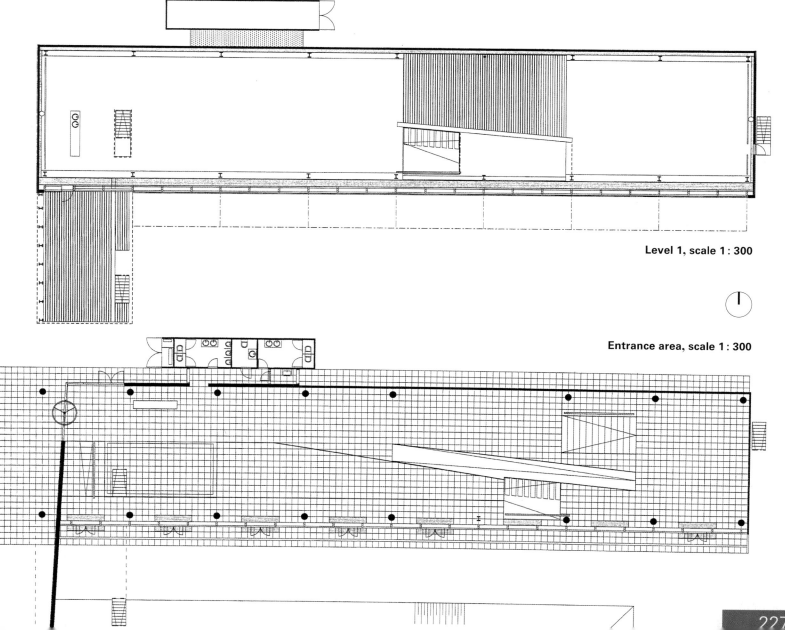

Level 1, scale 1 : 300

Entrance area, scale 1 : 300

Martin Wimmer

Subterranean Movements
In Earth Architecture

Earth Architecture

The end of the 20th century witnessed the onset of globalisation. Architecture was not unaffected by this. A sort of global adjustment developed. In other words: international facelessness. In contrast, examples of contemporary culture, subterranean structures for sport and leisure lead to an architectural movement which resists faceless global architecture through its distinctiveness.

For ecological reasons, 'earth-sheltered' buildings have been emerging since the 1980s with a view to creating an energy-conserving, humanitarian environment. Countless subterranean buildings have created a new 'green' architecture by visually minimising large building exteriors. Sculpturally formed 'earth architecture' – environmentally friendly large buildings – display a consolidated ecological development.

Highly developed technological buildings also bear the hallmarks of the new architectural movement: buildings which in an urban structure appear only as a rooftop, as an empty space (Berlin Velodrome and Swimming Complex,

The Berlin Velodrome and Swimming Complex, 1997/1999. Dominique Perrault

San Cataldo Cemetery in Modena
Aldo Rossi, 1971

Dominique Perrault, 1997/1999), or landscaped shells (Palais Omnisport de Paris-Bercy, Michel Andrault, Pierre Parat, Jean Prouvé, 1984) hinder city living. The disappearance of architecture under ground has triggered a new discussion on urban life.

Subterranean constructions date back thousands of years. They began with the building of burial chambers underneath the pyramids at Giza, and in the holy temples of Abu Simbel: great architecture – above ground. The dead were buried in underground catacombs (Rome, second century), or in the high walls of a necropolis (Aldo Rossi, San Cataldo, 1971).

However, the living pressed on underground. The route from the ancient open stadium, or even the municipal sports ground by Freidrich Ludwig Jahn (Berlin, 1811), through the inner world of the recently closed great hall (Rome Olympic Games, 1960, Palazzetto by Annibale Vitellozzi and Pier Luigi Nervi), to the technically advanced sports hall built into the rocks in Norway (Lillehammer Winter Olympics, 1994) once seemed almost unintelligible. A tendency of the world above towards that under ground has become apparent.

The Velodrome and swimming pool in Berlin marked a turning point in the conception of subterranean sports architecture: the urban architectural creation of space is no longer perceptible – the architecture is invisible. Landscape architecture is formalised – an orchard of 450 ornamental apple trees replaces the architecture in the case of the Velodrome in Berlin. Great architecture does not develop in this way.

Plato's famous cave allegory is 2370 years old. In the seventh book of his *Politeia* (*Republic*) he philosophised on the antithesis of the cave – as space and the temporal sensory world of man – and on the light as the genuine, objective world of ideas. At the beginning of the 20th century, 'light-air-sun' emerged as the leitmotif of a movement which demanded not only brighter, healthier flats, but also a departure from 'gloom' – from constriction, dankness, misery and general sadness.

In contrast, many architectural projects tend to involve in-earth or below ground works – down there where for a long time only mines, underground trains, underground car parks, sewers and bunkers were to be found. Huge halls were built for sport, concerts or other events, to accommodate several thousand people, although, according to statistics, over 20 per cent of people suffer from claustrophobia. The risks include disasters resulting from power cuts, water leakage, fire and structural collapse. Even though new techniques, power supplies and control systems benefit the production of underground projects, some of those who use the buildings nevertheless find existence in the depths psychologically problematic.

Major sporting events can last longer than six hours, and the capacity in underground buildings can reach 10,000. There are physical and emotional problems. 'Sick Building Syndrome' (SBS) is an underestimated human hazard caused by 'illness-inducing buildings' – regardless of whether they are built below or above ground. The causes of this condition are artificially ventilated or air-conditioned rooms. According to the World Health Organisation (WHO), SBS causes around one million cases of illness in Germany alone. Buildings which frequently trigger illness are those with thick outer shells and mechanical ventilation systems.

Assuming that Sick Building Syndrome could be countered by structural means (mechanical ventilation, artificial lighting), there remain the emotional or psychological problems, which can only be partially resolved. Fear of certain circumstances – phobias – are not the consequences of a genuine threat, but of a threat perceived as being real. The most common phobias include agoraphobia (fear of open spaces) and claustrophobia (fear of confined spaces). Both phobias can occur in underground buildings.

What has dragged sport, free time and recreational buildings down into the underworld after more than 6,000 years of urban building and architecture? How did the development of large buildings underground, which up to now were a determining factor of the townscape and provided architectural innovation, come about? How does this relate to 'sight,' if, according to Leonardo da Vinci, 'the eye is the universal judge of all things'? Are there no longer any secrets, if, according to Oscar Wilde, 'the secret of the world is the visible, not the invisible'?

Pressing functional requirements, similar to those in mining or vehicle manufacture, are not applicable if recreational buildings are located underground. Is this the relished creative approach which tempts the likes of Ieoh Ming Pei, Tadao Ando, Hans Hollein, Jörn Utzon, Christoph Langhoff, Dietz/Joppien/Joppien and Dominique Perrault to become subterranean architects?

It remains to be explained why architects plan large buildings underground, and whether this allows architecture to find new forms of expression. Are rooms with virtual windows – invisibly modifiable equivalent to cyberspace? To put it more simply, how can underground, mostly invisible buildings provide a new spatial environment capable of complementing, altering or renewing the existing environment? Will man be overlooked as the originator of all architectural activity in favour of a not entirely human (as the majority of humans are not irreplaceable) hi-tech development?

Subterranean buildings are spaceless from a town planning point of view, architecturally disembodied, artistically void and therefore expressionless. They stand in direct contrast to the emerging information society. So, does renunciation of stature and expression mean a renunciation of architecture altogether at the turn of a new century?

However, not all underground structures are entirely invisible; a distinction can be made between three spatial levels of the underworld: 'in earth', 'under earth' and 'underneath earth'. In parallel, there are two further categories: 'indoor' and 'open air'.

Berlin Olympic Stadium, 1936, with conversion plans for the 2006 World Cup, Stand 2000. gmp – Meinhard von Gerkan, Volkwin Marg and Partner Scale approx. 1 : 2 500

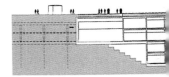

Apart from this craving for sensation, there are legitimate reasons for building into the ground: in a functional, economic and ecological way. Increasingly, more cities are forced to build underground due to a lack of building space. After the construction of underground train systems and car parks, there is an irresistible tendency towards underground cultural, sporting and recreational buildings .

When evaluating the 100 or so sport and recreational bulidings of the past 25 years, the first trends are already beginning to emerge:

1. Constructing sport and recreational buildings in urban areas dotted with nature is only feasible when current site density allows it.

2. Constructing sport and recreational buildings in high-rise-blocks has not yet been sufficiently researched; sports tower blocks – in Rotterdam and in several American cities – remain exceptional projects.

3. There exists a wide range of underground sports and recreational buildings, from urban integrated modern buildings to the conversion of existing natural or artificial hollows and tunnels.

Underground buildings – aspects and tendencies
1. Causes: lack of building land, obligations to preserve sites of historic value, use of topography, minimisation, security, conversion of existing buildings, conversion of mines.

2. Use: sports halls, indoor and open-air swimming pools, bowling alleys, fitness studios, dry ski slopes, cycling, canoeing, walking routes.

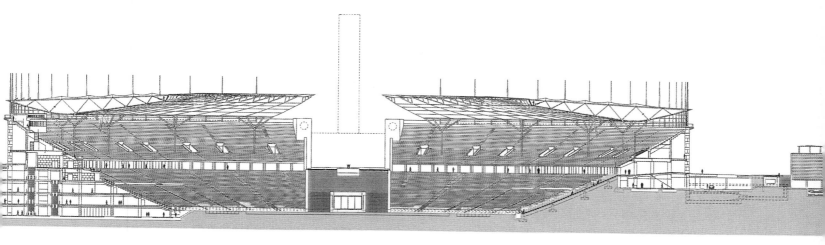

3. Ecology: 'more green – less hall', less sealing of surfaces, fulfilment of the International Olympic Committee requirement (1995) of 'greening the Olympics' as the third pillar of the Olympic ideal.

4. Shape: in a topographical context, to complement function and construction – in earth, under earth, underneath earth.

5. Town Planning: a loss of dominance by 'demonumentalising' down to an 'invisible city'.

6. Architecture: the range from a minimised, integrated architecture to an eliminated, architecture-less development.

7. Design: walls and roofs embanked, landscaped, earth sheltered.

8. Transformations: from glass façades to greenery, from façade architecture to interior achitecture, from traditional aesthetic to cave aesthetic.

Cultural buildings – examples and standards

For example, four projects are given whose construction posed comparable problems to those entailed by subterranean sports facilities construction (large capacity, development, environmental integration). Here, the requirements of heritage protection allow only below ground solutions.

1. Philharmonic Hall, Cologne (Peter Busmann, Godfried Harberer, 1986): the uninterrupted view from the Rhine to the cathedral had to remain.

2. The 'Kosmos' cinema, Berlin (Josef Kaiser, 1962, Konrad Beckmann, 1998). The view of the Hauptsaal completed in 1960, protected by heritage – a testimony to the former East Germany – had to be left as it was.

3. The Congress Hall, Florence (Paolo Spadolini, 1965): one of the world's first underground halls. They had to preserve the view of a listed palace and park.

4. The Louvre extension, Paris (Ieoh Ming Pei, Michael Marari, 1993): an above ground extension was not even considered.

Underground stadia

People have lived, worked and survived underground for thousands of years. Since the 20th century, underground locations have also been used for sporting and recreational events. An array of buildings and projects demonstrates whether these sports and recreational buildings are logical and consistent, or illogical and so dispensable.

The first underground sports and recreational structures were huge stadia. Structural dimensions necessitated solutions which either minimised or integrated volume. Three examples in Germany which won international acclaim are listed below:

1. The German Stadium, Berlin (Otto March, 1913), intended for the Berlin Olympic Games in 1916, which were cancelled because of the First World War: out of deference to the adjacent Grunewald racecourse, the largest stadium in the world at that time (666 metre cycling track, 600 metre running track, 100 metre swimming pool) was invisible, buried in a basin in the ground.

2. The Berlin Olympic Stadium, built for the XI Olympic Games in 1936: the stadium, constructed to hold around 100,000 spectators, was reduced to around half its external appearance in size due to the sunken grandstand. The architect, Werner March, therefore reduced Hitler's demand

for grandeur. The spatial effect of the stadium interior was enhanced by the topographical difference between the entrance at street level and the sunken pitch level.

3. The Münich Olympic Stadium (Behnisch and Partner, Frei Otto), constructed for the XX Olympic Games in 1972: an Olympic park was sited in the immediate vicinity of the city centre in an artificially created mountain, in which the stadium, sports hall and swimming pool were constructed. The concept was to absorb the particular atmosphere of Münich as the 'City of museums and art', and to restore the original sense and substance to the Olympic Games.

In Earth, under Earth, underneath Earth
During the 1990s, large sports halls were built underground at three levels: 'in earth' (Max-Schmeling-Halle, Berlin), 'under earth' (Velodrome and swimming pool, Berlin), and 'underneath earth' (sportshall and swimming pool, Gjoevik/Lillehammer). Other projects worldwide led to paradigms of a new evolutionary trend. They had considerably influenced the planning of sports and

recreational buildings. One unexpected side-effect was that they were regarded in the meantime as the communication centre of a new subterranean movement.

Indoor halls were then combined with open-air centres, 'on earth'. The topography of a hillside site provided opportunities to relocate large sections of the building underground. In the meantime, 'half in earth' is the ecological and economical worldwide standard, especially with school sports halls. Artificial sinking can be used to achieve this if no natural slope is available. First example, the sports hall in Landskrona (1966) by Arne Jacobsen.

The large OmniSport sports hall in Paris-Bercy, part of an extensive urban sports and recreational centre, demonstrates a partial sinking within a total embankment. An 'in earth' solution was chosen to tone down its otherwise huge dimensional appearance. The hall was partially lowered, and the side walls were embanked with earth and planted with grass. This created a new type of shape of the 'earth

XX Olympic Games, Münich, 1972.
Behnisch and Partner, Frei Otto

sheltered' buildings. The steep 45 degree gradient required special lawn-mowing and maintenance apparatus. Façades in their conventional form no longer exist.

The athletics hall at the Horst Korber Sports Centre in Berlin (Langhof/Hänni/Meerstein, 1990) and the 'bath house' at the Spreewaldplatz, also in Berlin (Christoph Langhof, 1987) are also triangularly located 'in earth'. The sports hall was not permitted to encroach on the view of the Olympic Stadium, with its heritage listing, and so was lowered into the ground; the swimming pool had to blend into the existing structure of the ample site – it was also partially sunken.

The Max Schmeling Hall in Berlin (Dietz/Joppien/Joppien, 1997) is half built into the earth, and integrated into the landscape of the Jahn sports park and surrounding residential area using adjoining halls covered with earth.

At the Hamburg-Halstenbek sports hall by André Poitier, the hall and adjoining rooms, i.e. the entire building, are located 'under earth'. Only the glass dome is visible.

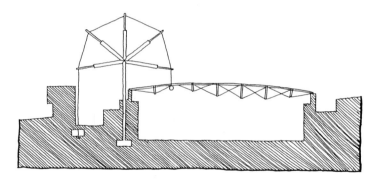

Horst Korber Sports Centre for competitive sport, Berlin, 1990. Christoph Langhof, Thomas M. Hänni, Herbert Meerstein

Max-Schmeling-Halle, Berlin, 1997. Dietz/Joppien/Joppien

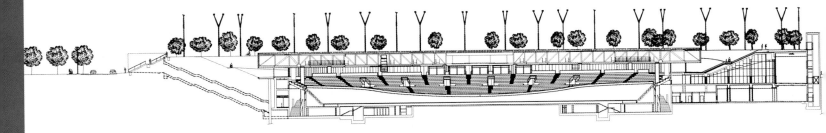

Longitudinal section of the Velodrome
Berlin, 1997. Dominique Perrault, scale 1 : 1 000

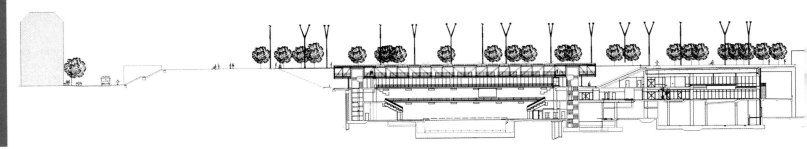

Cross section of the swimming pool
Berlin, 1999. Dominique Perrault, scale 1 : 1 000

The Forum des Halles in Paris (1987) was constructed as a complex building for trade, catering, sport and leisure, recreation, art and culture, fashion and literature, and is connected to the outskirts by the new RER Metro fast train network. As a borderline case between 'under earth' and 'underneath earth', the opening into a courtyard shows that typologically consistent solutions are not practicable. To put it more positively – only the architectural profile concentrated on the courtyard allows urban space to develop, and associates this with the urban texture.

The Velodrome and swimming pool, Berlin (1997/1999): in conjunction with the (failed) Berlin bid to host the 2000 Olympic Games, a surprisingly radical solution was reached as the result of a competition for a velodrome and swimming pool. The Parisian architect, Dominique Perrault, suggested two huge sports halls be entirely sunken into the ground, to be implemented with very little alteration to the landscape.

This marked a pivotal turning point in sports and recreational construction, observed worldwide – from great hall architecture to landscape architecture, from monumental construction to filigree roof structure, from accumulated architectural design to 'land art'. These large buildings built into the ground up to the rooftop were a bold step on the route to the underground. Only the huge roofs coated in chrome-plated steel – similar to shimmering lakes – remained visible. Landscaped embankments with steps suggest that the building will soon be covered with an orchard of 450 apple trees.

The chances of duplicating this design seem fairly slim due to fire and security protection requirements.

Genuine 'underneath earth' – i.e. wholly invisible underground sports buildings – were developed in Norway, where they were built into the rocks by miners. In Oslo, the sports hall and swimming pool were built in Holmlia (1983), and in Lillehammer/Gjoevik, a sports hall and swimming pool were built for the 1994 Winter Olympics. This radical solution of halls built into rocks was the result of several requirements: large sports halls had to be constructed without the use of building land, they also had to accumulate gravel for road construction and create shelters for protection against nuclear weapons, which could be used as emergency hospitals in the event of a war.

The benchmark tests of these Norwegian experiments conducted by experts are inconclusive. The fear of claustrophobia in underground buildings, inadequate emergency exits, and the smallest possible architectural profile reduced to a mere three entrance gates are the arguments of those opposed. Those in favour counter these citing optimal energy saving, constant temperature and reduced costs. These sports constructions built into the rocks are not paradigmatic of an 'internal architecture' yet to be redetermined, as they are invisible, without evident interaction with the cityscape and self-sufficient.

Planning and building cultural, sports and recreational buildings (in conjunction with sports facilities), in accordance with new guidelines, in valuable natural landscapes, in heavily urbanised city centres or in new suburban centres is unavoidable. The aim of preserving natural space, or the lack of suitable land in cities forces architecture underground. Underground swimming pools such as the Hungarian baths in Miskolo-Tapolca demonstrate an internationally evolving trend for 'in earth' and 'under earth' buildings.

Hotel and recreational facilities in conjunction with sophisticated spa architecture can use the particular underground effect to their advantage. And so the romance of a well-formed hilly landscape with underground freshwater caves and waterfalls in Bad Gastein has become part of an 'architectural landscape', conforming to new standards. It is conceivable that the Norwegian experiences of rock building development and security techniques could be evaluated and applied for future use in existing and artificially created caverns located in disused potash and salt mines.

A disused potash mine in Sonderhausen (Thuringia) was converted into an adventure park. Sporting activities are planned in the 25-kilometre long underground passageways and tunnels at depths of up to 700 metres: boat trips along saline lakes, mountain bike trails on tunnel tracks, a 6-mile long ice skating track, and a probably record-breaking climbing wall. Claustrophobia gives way to vertigo.

Velodrome, Berlin, 1997/2000. Dominique Perrault

Ulrich Stock

Body and Rock
A thermal spring of natural stone in the
Swiss mountain village of Vals
Peter Zumthor

Tension, exhaustion and fatigue are good reasons to visit Vals, but not for the drive there, as the abyss gapes before the driver for the last 20 kilometres of the mountain road. This is why you are recommended to fly to Zürich, travel by train to Ilanz, then by mail bus to Vals. Such a palaver costs money; it is a luxurious feeling as a sense of well-being starts setting in on your way there; while changing from one form of transport to another and standing around waiting for it to arrive, you come to realise that you are actually reaching a corner of the world which is in the middle of Europe.

Vals is in Switzerland, with 1000 inhabitants, at the mouth of the long Vals valley, only 3000 more behind it and then Ticino. A quiet mountain village situated at 1250 metres above sea level: skiing in winter, hiking in summer – nothing especially different from the many Swiss alpine villages. But for the thermal spring located in the rocks there.

It would be nice to say that it is world famous, and this would hardly be an exaggeration. People in the know head for the Vals thermal spring from all over Europe; even Japanese and Americans have been sighted entering this unique spa, fascinated by its ultra-smooth, grey-greenish rock faces, its railings made from brushed brass, its curtains of heavy, black leather and its illuminated, sharply right-angled caverns!

No well-travelled person comes here by chance. They have read, heard, perhaps even found out on the television about this building which places stone and water and air and light in a relationship as archaic as it is abstract. Enthusiasts of architecture can be found lying stretched out. After hardly any time at all, they fall on their knees, even lie down on the ground in order to read the cracks of the building as if they were a Bible. The 'Zumthor Book' – a revelation!

Peter Zumthor: the architect who is also responsible for the museum in Bregenz, the Swiss Expo-Pavilion in Hanover, and the 'Topography of Terror' museum in Berlin, the latter controversial due to its cost. The thermal spring at Vals officially opened a good three years ago, and is Zumthor's masterpiece. It cost the municipality of Vals 26 million Swiss francs, approximately 18 million Euros; its spectacular success became the model for upmarket tourism: contemporary architecture made from the place for the place, an aesthetic memorial contrary to anything average, mainstream – and the temple of a meditative spa culture.

The black-painted tunnel which leads into the thermal spring in the rocks is not even two metres high, and is quite narrow. There would have been more room, but the message to the visitor is made clear right from the entrance: from here, you are entering the interior of the rock, the 'self'. Here, you become a caveman.

It is straight ahead to the changing rooms, past windowless concrete which faces towards the mountain. Brass pipes jut out from which runs what is known in the city supermarket as mineral water. Here, it is still untreated, unfiltered, naturally loaded with ionized iron which coats the ground daily with an ever-increasing reddish brown patina. A sediment which tells of time gone by, of the power of the constant dripping. Then it is time for changing, and wow! cubicles! almost cabins! The lockers are made from red mahogany, the benches from black leather. Take me with you into the thermal spring, captain! The time it takes to slip out of your suit and into your bathrobe becomes a ritual: ceremonial preparation for what is to come. You do not dawdle to the spa, you walk tall!

The principle is so simple: out of the windowless rock into the light. On the one hand, there are spa caves full of corners which are deprived of sunlight; on the other hand, there are giant, high windows on three sides overlooking the valley. Between them are stonewalled columns which sometimes grant, and sometimes bar, the view to the visitor. Every position offers yet another combination of light and stone. And even if you do not move from that spot which marks your damp feet on the floor plate, you will constantly see something different: this is because the immense slabs of concrete of the indoor ceiling do not square up to each other, but rather form crevices into which sunlight falls at a constantly changing angle.

Craftsmen would be the perfect complement to the architectural public. For a few days, they would not have to drill, screw, plug, bend anything straight, and not lie down in a constricted position; but rather, they could drift, half-heartedly tinker and be amazed at how people can also build. No pipes. No grating. No signposts. No shafts. No glazed tiles. No man-made doors. No silicone joints. No DIY jobs.

Instead, the walls: layer upon layer of natural stone slabs in three varying strengths which run through the house and give it an inner rhythm. Coarse grained gneiss from Vals, blasted from the rock in the nearby village quarry, cut to the exact millimetre by the most modern machines, and processed so precisely by brick-layers that 50-metre long joints around all corners and edges move through the building at exactly the same height.

Most photographs of the thermal spring show only these walls, the water and the light, but when you are there you will also see people. If there are only a few, then the interplay between stone and body unfolds: the perpetual rock, the transitory human being. You can then become very intimidated by the power of the architecture – or even euphoric: this is where earthly fulfilment becomes a reality.

When everything is right, you become more aware. Bikinis and swimming trunks become an obstacle to proper immersion as though they were protective clothing from the commercial world weakening the existential contrast between rock and skin. You would have to bathe naked – but that is not allowed.

You must protect this sumptuous experience from any interference. Against the he-men who splash and shout around their conquests as if they were in a leisure pool. Against the elderly who mutter constantly as if in the waiting room of Dr. Death. Pssst!

Whether you are experiencing the fully automatic whirlpool baths with their mountain view, or the vigour of a full-body aromatherapy massage – it is quite clear that this is nothing like the conventional health spa business and the cures offered by stingy insurance companies. This is an esoteric healing concept which matches the philosophy of the place. After a meeting between stone walls, Indian tea is served from the bag which has promises of luck printed on it. So, not everything is perfect; a number of things in the construction are, though. But prices have gone through the roof and would indicate that visitors are more likely to be architects than craftsmen.

The hotel is clearly not up to the standards of the thermal spring; until recently, it even had a bad reputation, which could be put down to the high-rise building built at the end of the 1960s and the forced alpine friendliness inside it. In the last few months, a few things have changed – less physical than spiritual changes, and that has a lot to do with the new management: Annalisa Zumthor, wife of the architect who designed the thermal spring, actually a professional teacher at a special school, and Claudia Knapp, television reporter. Neither knew anything about the tourism industry when they started at the end of October 1999. We will be able to see the impact this has on finances later on, but the effect on the guests has already become apparent. Two eloquent ladies who prefer to read books rather than balance sheets, who are enthusiastic about music and art, and who with their charm brighten up even that poky room which is still fitted out with folding beds.

They do not want the best possible management of a poor state of affairs; they want to bring the hotel up to the standard of the thermal spring. Eleven of the 140 rooms have already been renovated with the help of the Zumthor architect. Cement floors painted white, blue-black carpets, Thai silk curtains, linen bed sheets, bedside tables designed by Zumthor, and instead of a television set, which is available only on express request, there is a CD-player with four CDs: Miles Davis, Dino Saluzzi, Ludwig von Beethoven, Fritz Hauser. Who is Fritz Hauser? He is the Swiss drummer who plays that hypnotic music on sound stones which can be heard in a far corner of the thermal spring. And which can also be heard when someone phones the hotel and is connected to an extension. So, everything comes together.

Guests on half-board can begin the day with freshly prepared muesli, and end it in the evening with six high-quality courses before retiring to the 1960s' style piano bar where, naturally, traditional jazz can be heard in between cover versions of well-known Swiss songs. People are amazed by this, and by the heterogeneous audience. The very rich, artists and art lovers, the young. From elegant folk in evening wear to those sampling the buffet at the bar in sauna slippers and jogging bottoms. That this great variety is accepted without demur is something which can only really be explained by the levelling power of the thermal spring: in the water, everyone gains a sense of what really counts in life.

A spring of your own
How Vals came by its thermal spring

A magnificent building does not fall from the sky; it grows out of the ground, and the ground must be made ready for it. So, how did a remote mountain village get hold of a world-renowned architect? Why did it fork out so much money for such a crazy idea, when a normal project would have been so much cheaper?

Two names provide the answer to the questions: Pius Truffer and Peter Schmid. Two men from Vals in the prime of life, friends – one owns a quarry, the other is a writer and a shepherd. When the municipality bought the old, bankrupt spa grounds in 1983 in order to build something new, they pressed for things not to be done by halves. They did not want the umpteenth copy of a Central European adventure spa; but rather something completely individual to adorn their valley. They had this idea and sufficient determination to stick to it – against the advice of every management consultant and marketing expert who advocated solutions that were too cheap for good money.

Truffer and Schmid looked for an architect and found Peter Zumthor who was not so well known at that point. Zumthor demanded that he should be trusted, and that he should not have to operate with committees. This self-assurance which bordered on arrogance did not deter the two men from Vals. It confirmed for them that they had found their man.

While Zumthor drew up the plans, Truffer and Schmid got down to the task of spreading enthusiasm for their ambitious project through the majority of villagers, as there is no council in Vals, just the citizens' assembly, or open council. A lot of voting had to be got through – and was.

A miracle that lasted 13 years. In 1996, after the opening of the thermal spring, the second miracle took place: the economic success exceeded all expectations. Today, Truffer and Schmid's preoccupation is to control the stream of visitors.

Peter Stürzebecher

Art Room – Sports Room
Work in Progress by Tadashi Kawamata
Bathing Resort in Zug by Alfred Krähenbühl

The Japanese artist, Tadashi Kawamata, pursued a long-term project from 1996 to 1999 in Zug (Switzerland). The outcome was a series of useable wooden handcraft – footbridges, bathing huts, terraces. Located along the waterfront and through the old town, they form an artistic pathway which ends or begins in the art house, depending on which way you look at it. Within the framework of a pioneering collective project, the museum had invited the artist to take part in a project which has been going on for several years, which is not concerned with acquisition of material possessions, but rather with the creation of an artistic process in a public space. The philosophy of the 1960s dictates that the broadened notion of the museum should be in accordance with the expanded notion of art. We quote here the words of Matthias Haldemann, director of the art house in Zug and initiator of this exceptionally courageous project:

'Kawamata, famous for his spectacular outside installations, accepted the offer eagerly and began a game of action-reaction with the population. In the small town which had been changing from a provincial place (between Lucerne and Zürich) into a commercial metropolis since 1970, no spectacular gesture comes as a surprise; the silent, sustainable work of Kawamata provides another point of view.'

With simple measures, the artist targeted the mindset of the inhabitants. Untreated, quickly ageing wood is only rarely used in a public area. The works require regular maintenance; otherwise, the woodwork will need to be removed after a few years – not many people like this. Makeshift solutions are also technical, such as intermediate stages in the construction or dismantling.

The functionality of the path is very popular. People enjoy the shade, areas for lounging on or for having a picnic, running tracks for joggers, beach volleyball stands, and the bathing resort designed by Alfred Krähenbühl.

Art promotes well-being. Users are a part of the open work and imperceptibly become the observer as the objects show them the familiar surroundings in a new light: the frameworks encompass real images of reality. You alight, so to speak, after a set period of time, are gently lifted up, led onto the water, guided as if suspended over platforms, and then a playful lightness overcomes you. On the station-like path, art-curious visitors stroll through the town which used to be only a museum, confronted by problems of public space as well.

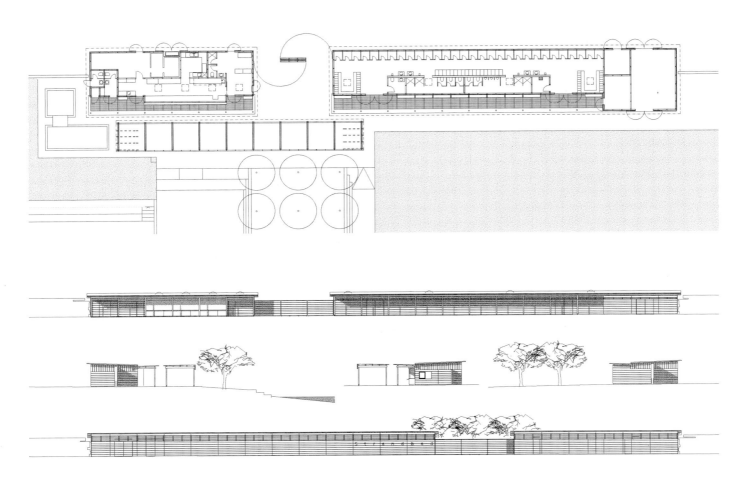

Ground plan and views of the bathing resort in Zug, 1998. Alfred Krähenbühl. Scale 1 : 500

Bathing resort in Zug, 1998. Alfred Krähenbühl

The functional objects along the way-station-like path become metaphors for art: the path is the goal, and stands for life. The person who strides along it becomes aware of movement as a river of life. Even the water on whose edge all activities settle is an ancient symbol for it.

Kawamata's subtle interventions bring together nature, town, human being and art along rigid edges, and literally prove to be transitional crossings.

'Work in Progress' stimulated increasingly wider repercussions over the years, and soon set the whole town in motion. The unemployed, school children, tradesmen, and even the army helped with the construction free of charge; the artist received private and public commissions, and his work is still the talk of the town.
Tadashi Kawamata's involvement led to an artistic and social 'Work in Progress'. In the course of this, the art house in Zug found its new model of a networked museum.

Tadashi Kawamata

'Kawamata's woodway appears to add nothing to, or even take away anything from the spaces in which he operates. He opens up space where there was none before', says Adolf Muschg on 'The Beauty of the Woodway' by Tadashi Kawamata.

The walls and the ten bathing huts arranged randomly in the grounds by Tadashi Kawamata are included in the bathing resort. The walls, roughly constructed by craftsmen from untreated wood, show the ageing process of the material and its perishability.

In contrast, the precise, well thought-out and physically coherent wooden construction of the bathing resort demonstrates a long lifespan to us. The 'chaotic plank layout' of the walls designed by Kawamata and the rather laid-back impression given by the

bathing huts (for changing, sitting, playing and passing time in) stand, in their spontaneous character, in contrast to the well-calculated wood-frame architecture of the bathing resort.

The compactness of the bathing resort confronts Kawamata with an anarchic maze of planks. Nevertheless, the measurements of the bathing resort building can be found again in the wooden wall. The wooden work by Alfred Krähenbühl and Kawamata's work using wood confront us in two languages – and in both, we recognise our own voices.

Peter Stürzebecher

Architecture Room – Sports Room
Bath House for Saint Nazaire by Sven Liebrecht

The former fishing village of Saint Nazaire is situated on the Breton Atlantic coast. The future location of shipyards and industry was completely destroyed in the Second World War under German occupation, and was converted into a submarine base which meant a dramatic break in the development of the town. With the new beginning after 1945, because of its ideal location a fruitful rivalry developed between the shipping industry which had meanwhile taken off, and the rapidly growing tourism at the furthest end of the Loire. For the shipyard workers of the place as well as for the travel-mad tourists, the 'bath house' at the outermost end of the harbour jetty of Saint Nazaire was supposed to promote relaxation, calm and to invite marine adventures.

The harbour jetty leads through to the bath house and divides it into two unequally large areas. The entrance area, sauna, technical department and café are located towards the sheltered harbour basin, and turned towards the open sea are the hall with swimming pools, screens for changing behind, and eight 'water houses'.

The author of the work, Sven Liebrecht, develops within the framework of a French-German seminar a precise idea about the motion sequences in the interior of the art room-sports room, about the architectural game of spatial emptiness and sculptural physicality, about the composition of light supply and perception, and about the experience which lends meaning to it:

'Sports Campus Saint Nazaire',
German-French Seminar 1999.
Technical High School, Hamburg and
School of Architecture, Nantes.
Peter Stürzebecher, Jacques Dulieu

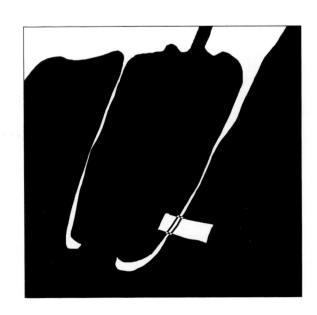

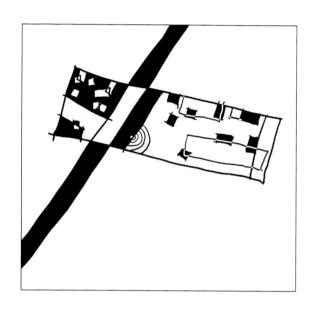

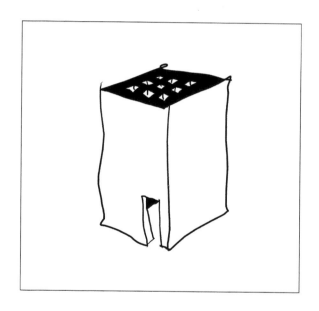

'Bathers make their way along a path which leads them out further and further into the sea. When bathers reach the bath house, they are already immersed in the expanse, in the interplay of light. Inside, this path is repeated towards the light; it leads from the mystical half-light of the saunas to the bright, clear light of the wide hall. Eight water houses set in a spatial continuum lead a double life: devoted to the different manifestations of the water, the spatial bodies – water houses – are cut out of the solid block of the sauna area (subtraction), leave their negative form there, and are pitched freely in the hall (addition) a few steps further as positive bodies. They stand in the room like human beings, in relation to each other and positioned towards the outside. The remaining negative form

becomes an adventure space turned inwards which invites the visitor to contemplate and meditate.

The water houses bring together the sensory experience of water, light and sound:

The water house as a room with a raging, cold waterfall and cascading, widely strewn light from the fanlights in the ceiling, the water house as an ice house with warmly splashing water and razor-sharp light pervading the room from the ceiling through a slit, the waterhouse as a room of rest with soft, diffuse light in which the person resting shares the view of the illuminated banks of the Loire with the sun.

The addition of the eight spatial bodies leads to a frequently changing atmosphere without destroying the spatial unity of the entire hall. The methodical (design) approach goes beyond the boundaries of functionalistic restrictions. Rooms whose interior and exterior seem to contradict each other invite discovery and a full-on experience. Experiencing becomes an experience.' (Sven Liebrecht)

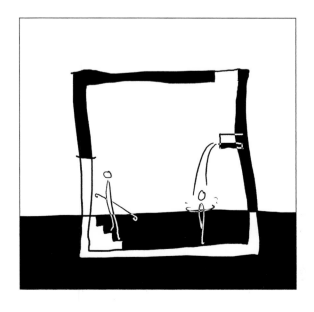

Peter Stürzebecher, Sigrid Ulrich

Asphalt Sport
A private appearance in the urban space

A few pairs of asphalt-friendly trainers can tell tales. Joschka Fischer's rise from school drop-out and taxi driver to political luminary is inextricably linked with the spectacle of his swearing-in ceremony in the Bundestag. Relaxed in trainers and casually dressed, he took the oath of office as a minister for the first time in 1985.

Today, Joschka Fischer's trainers are exhibited in the leather museum in Offenbach as cult objects. The consequences of the sporty modern society can hardly have a better example. The increase in value of the body and of its covering – sports clothes – triggered a body and leisure boom, which rebounded right into the midst of the pinstripe-clad crowd.

The pursuit of the body beautiful and the design of the corresponding sporty covering – or uncovering – has become fashionable with the Monday to Friday toiling crowd as well as with the corporate image hierarchies. The struggle for a muscular physique no longer rages in clubs, conventional sports halls, running tracks, and on traditional sports and playing fields; but rather in cities, in street backyards or on the magnificent boulevard.

The new repertoire of jogging, free climbing, mountain biking, adventure sport, American football, hang-gliding, basketball or rollerblading has become a status symbol and longs for publicity.

Sport was mainly reserved for men until the 1960s. The fitness semantics of women's aerobics as a new exercise culture in an erotic outfit has since then opposed the masculine way of 'making their mark'. A boundary-free, sexually indeterminate individuality is gaining acceptance in sport by offering a lot of variety. Social patterns are breaking up; even the urban space is affected by it.

Just like silent resistance fighters, rollerbladers skate unheard over asphalt and road surfaces, wind their way between cars and people on streets and footpaths. Open spaces which would be inconceivable for car drivers to negotiate in traffic are conquered elegantly. The feeling of having limitless experiences becomes apparent when the street becomes the stage with the help of a well-designed transport device, fashionable clothes, and loud music blaring in the background.

With skateboards, rollerblades and bicycles, new norms are emerging for the person on the move. Urban spaces – streets, playing fields, parks – encourage a performance in front of an increasingly interested audience. It arouses a festive atmosphere even in the spectator when – as with the city marathon in Berlin, Hamburg, New York, Paris or elsewhere – sport lures the crowds into collective involvement.

Asphalt and road surfaces unite everyone and give everyone, through sports fashion, the chance to be 'involved' in a public area. To experience team sport privately in public is the answer to the increasing demands of the working world with a performance hierarchy, constant pressures of time, and a fast-paced environment. The sensory perception which gets diluted in the city between offices and limousines which are largely soundproofed, air-conditioned and sheltered in glass with anti-glare shields, comes back via the asphalt.

The participation of people who live in urban isolation becomes both chance and compulsion with asphalt sport as the informality of the 'sporty looking' participant and of the 'sporty feeling' spectator carries a price:
Performance wants to be developed in a dual sense.

Expensive cycling machines, scooters, combinations of rollerblades and prams are obstacles to the indiscriminate participation of everybody in the new street sport. The trend for brand names – for instance, with sports wear and sports shoes – as an instrument of de-levelling is already highly developed in children. And sport, dance and other physical activities have for a long time now been playing dutiful servant to the master of the expected social goals of youthfulness and slenderness.

The sculpted and 'look-at-me' physique is becoming the projection surface in the media age. The exposure of the physique which has been honed by sport faces us every day on the street, and not only on a large scale when Wonder Bras and boxer shorts are being advertised. Training and fitness programmes, forms of treatment right up to surgical snips and a distinct fashion approach become a prerequisite for participation in the public scene. Perhaps one's own development and public acceptance in the urban space are only attainable as a result of physical fine-tuning which has been worked at in the gym.

But it looks as though the real, youthful participants are already a giant step ahead of the hard-trying crowd, with ten year-olds throwing themselves up against building walls in acrobatic feats on wooden boards, rotating 360 degrees by jumping at a dizzy height and then landing back on the ground looking cool, and casually changing course on the asphalt with a feeling of irrepressible *joie de vivre*.

Stéphane Courarie-Delage

La Ville comme Stade – Paris

Reportage

Ulrich Pramann

A Magical Place Called 'Stadium'

The entire city becomes an arena, a stage. A stage for me, an arena for all the others. The approximately 34 000 others probably see it in a similar way. Each of them has previously run many kilometres, many lonely hours by themselves. Country roads, woodland paths, suburban streets, who knows where. And today, the grand entrance in this large, this magnificent city.

New York City Marathon. For runners, there is nothing that could be more enticing; to have this immense arena, this splendid city as a stage. New York belongs to the runners for hours; on this

day, they dictate the pace in the City. Hectic traffic remains shut out for hours. The City assumes a different form. The runner plays the main role. And today, every marathon runner has the one-off chance to feel like the leading man or lady.

What a backdrop. The architecture – breathtaking. Of course, everyone knows the main buildings from pictures. Right in the middle of them though, 'live', everything is initially truly breathtaking. Breathtaking. A November wind whistles through the gaps between buildings. You feel so small in this setting and

yet so grand in these endlessly long moments to which you have been looking forward for such a long time. You have to run over five bridges, through five districts. Starting place is Staten Island, then Brooklyn, Queens, the Bronx, finally Manhattan. First Avenue, lastly a section of Fifth Avenue. The finishing line is in Central Park.

Was that a celebration?! Me, right in the middle of it. An experience, an adventure, a triumph I will never forget. About two million people on the roadside. Oh boy! How they spurred us on enthusiastically and gaily accompanied us, how they gave every individual in the throng the feeling that everybody was there just because of them: 'Hey, you're a star, you're the greatest!' How that gives you the drive to carry on. What an arena! How wonderful the New York crowd is, how infectious their enthusiasm is! The people of New York – they encourage you. And they play music. – In Brooklyn, it is black, addictive. In Queens, bands drum. In the Bronx, ghettoblasters sit on window ledges, they inspire you with the theme music of *Chariots of Fire* – a poignant glorification of 1920s running idols.

I fear the onset of a low ebb, this terrible, almost endless strain. But I also look forward to deliverance in Central Park. And a few kilometres beforehand, these strong feelings of happiness really do come, feelings which run over your back like a shiver and bring tears to your eyes.

Magic moments. Strong impressions which are stored in my memory forever. And the nicest thing of all: like a wonderful film, I can replay them within me whenever I want.

City marathon, Paris 2000

Think of the finishing-line above all. Central Park. On this day, it was an improvised stadium which lured umpteen thousands of people. They get close up so they can look in the faces of happy heroes. And you are one of them.

How are you actually supposed to enter a proper stadium? I have even been in an Olympic stadium a few times. In Athens, for example, it was disappointing. Perhaps because the expectations were so high. Attempting to follow in the footsteps of the legends of the first marathon (1896). And then this *tristesse* of the Greek metropolis which almost completely ignored us runners and exposed us to the stench and noise of the city traffic.

I liked the setting in München a lot better. The best, best, best moment of all: when, after almost 42 kilometres, you run, flagging, through a tunnel and at the end of this tunnel, you are almost at the finishing-line. But, first, you pick up the 'live' stadium atmosphere for yourself. This time, not as a spectator, no, as an athlete! In which other discipline do you get this? You are a participant in a large field with world-class athletes, and, like a world-class athlete, you too run into the stadium. Into the Olympic stadium! And your loved ones are sitting on the stands, and they are proud.

But no one can be as proud as you at this moment in time.

All athletes feel the same way at such a moment, even major athletes who write sports history. On the day before the first Olympic race in which women were allowed to take part, Joan Benoit had to go to the loo almost once every hour. She could not sleep. She lay in bed and listened over and over again to the stimulating Vangelis film music from *Chariots of Fire* on her Walkman. Then she would sleep for an hour. She would dream. She would dream that she was locked up in a department store and that someone had forgotten her.

Sunday, 5 August 1984. There is no detail of this day that Joan Benoit will ever forget. Like how her insides were still giving her trouble. How, like officials, the 50 female marathon runners from 28 countries were led into the stadium shortly before 8 in the morning, and how they were sorted alphabetically according to country and height. How she, the smallest, stood at the end of the group. Runners like telling stories about their best race in which everything seemed to be quite easy.

For Joan Benoit, the Olympic marathon was one of these races. The race almost ran itself.
Not far from the finishing-line, she saw herself. Her sponsor, Nike, had had a massive, larger-than-life picture painted on a building wall: Joan Benoit at her brilliant 1983 victory in Boston.

And then there was the tunnel, looming ahead, which led into the memorial stadium.

Her mother later said that Joan, when she ran into the Olympic stadium, had looked like a small, grey mouse venturing timidly out of its hole. At this great moment, the daughter had quite different thoughts. She knew: 'Now your whole life will change.'

Her legs felt like rubber. She bowed her head and said to herself: 'You are not there yet, just run another lap!' But of course, she had finished. In the last 200 metres, she waved happily and removed her cap. Shortly before the finishing-line, someone handed her a flag with the Stars and Stripes, and the crowd almost flipped when their petite compatriot, Joan Benoit, ran the last metres to the finishing-line. In the stadium 80 000 people saw Joan crying with happiness.

Small happiness, big happiness and collective feelings of happiness which come up quite suddenly and erupt like a volcano. Thousands of spectators, tens of thousands, who act as

if drunk on happiness and transmogrify into riotous, screaming, spluttering, hugging children in their rapture – this is only possible on this scale in a concrete basin called a stadium.

For example: Argentina, 1978. The World Cup final. Scraps of material and paper and confetti flew around, more than at all the carnivals in Cologne put together. The Argentinian colours of light blue and white were everywhere. Like a lady's smock in the wind, the stadium broke out into waves as soon as something happened on the pitch. And when the hosts finally defeated Holland, the thunderous enthusiasm rose to a Vamos-Argentina orgy. As a journalist I was privileged to be right in the middle of it at that time. Never again would I feel such an electrically charged, goose-pimply atmosphere.

Not even in 1996 in Atlanta when Michael Johnson drummed the tartan track, in long swift strides, the upper part of his body held

as a stiff as a poker, and won his 400 metre gold medal after setting a new record time (43.49 secs.). The 83 000-strong crowd leapt to their feet, went wild, and paid homage to the US star with a standing ovation. In this moment, Michael embodied the perfect athlete for whom everything ran perfectly. It seemed as if the movement analyses which took years to perfect from a computer, the shape optimisations from the wind-tunnel, the material developments from the chemical laboratory were all tailor-made for him and had produced the perfect result. It seemed as though the architects themselves had built Atlanta's stadium just for him, had developed this special tartan mix just for him.

Everything seemed like the production of a triumphant moment worth a few thousand million. And Michael Johnson represented the ideal of a moulded athlete of the future.

Only the dimensions of the track did not seem transcendental, but rather as they always are and probably will always remain – exactly 400 metres.

The Olympic Games, Sydney 2000

Performance test in the wind-tunnel

Regarding my pictures

'I work as a painter and scientist in Hamburg. Both occupations are equal for me. Whenever I overdo it in one of them, the urge always arises to achieve a balance with the other. The preoccupation with the human being recurs in both. Especially the behaviour of the human being among his/her fellow men and women.

The everyday experiences are assimilated and converted into a metaphorical language.

As a suitable means of expression, I used a greatly reduced representational depiction right to the limits of abstraction. Individual figures report on their way of living. Several individuals, different from each other, and yet the same in essence, result in a sequence when seated behind one another. A part of my self-portrait and a part of my counterpart features in all of the figures.

In this sense, one can and is supposed to identify with oneself and also with others when observing my paintings. I hope people derive a lot of pleasure from this.'

Appendix

Project Catalogue Short Biographies Index of Architects
Index of Photographers Index of Projects

Udo Dietrich.
The Stilt Walkers,
Hamburg, 2000
Stained painting on acrylic glass,
30 x 26 cm

Catalogue of Projects

Structural design: René R. Guillod, WGG
Engineers AIA/ASIC,
Photographer: Gaston Wicky

Architect: David Chipperfield
Structural design: Structural Engineers
Whitby, Bird and Partners
Design of outside area/landscape:
Whitelaw Turkington
Photographer: Dennis Gilbert/View

Page 224
Netherlands Sports Museum
Type of building: museum and institute
Use: exhibition
Location: Lelystad, the Netherlands
Completion: 1995
Architect: Victor Mani
Structural design: D. H. V. Bouw BV
Photographers: Stijn Brakee, Jannis
Linders, Daria Scagliola

Projects from the Specialist Contributions

Page 34
Nike:
Client: Nike Inc.,
Beaverton/Oregon, USA
Architects: Thompson Vaivoda and
Associates Architects AIA, Portland/OR
Interior designers: Williamson/McCarter,
Portland/OR
Civil engineers: W & H Pacific,
Beaverton/OR
Landscape designers: Mayer/Reed,
Portland/OR, Murase Associates, Port-
land/OR, Richard Haag Associates,
Seattle/WA, Bob Mazany, Beaverton/OR
(trees) SRI/Shapiro/AGCO, Portland/
OR (biotopes and marshland)
David Evans & Associates, Portland/OR
(biotopes and marshland)

Signposts: Ambrosi Design Ltd.,
Portland/OR
Graphics: JoMac Graphic
Communications, Alameda/CA
Audiovisuals: EIS, Inc., Sacramento/CA
Geotechnique: AGRA, Portland/OR
Acoustics: McKay Conant Brook, Inc.,
Westlake Village/CA, USA

Page 36
Reebok:
Client/project developer: Reebok
International Ltd and Credit Suisse
Architects: NBBJ, Seattle/WA, Scott
Wyatt, Steven Mc Connell, K. Robert
Swartz, Jonathan Ward, Jin Ah Park,
Nick Charles
Interior designers: NBBJ Seattle/WA,
Alan Young, Chris Larson, Dave Burger
Structural engineers: McNamara/Salvia,
Inc., Boston/MA, Robert McNamara,
Joseph Salvia
Landscape designers: EDAW, Seattle/
WA, Robert Shrosbee, Ed Mah, Kathy
Kirby
Traffic planning: Vanasse Hangen Brust-
lin, Inc., Watertown/MA, Steve
Thomas
Design consultants: Turner/O,Conner,
Boston/MA, Bob Keaffer, Sonia
Richards, Peter Johnson
Domestic technique: Cosentini Associates,
Cambridge/MA Richard Leber
General Counsel: Reebok International
Ltd. Corporate General Counsel, Canton/
MA, Barry Nagler, Ropes & Gray, Boston/
MA

Page 38
adidas:
Client: World of Sports: adidas-
Salomon AG, Herzogenaurach, Germany
Prize giver of the 'Urban Developmental
competition' and awarding authority
Master plan: GEV Grundstücksentwick-
lungsgesellschaft mbH & Co. KG,
Herzogenaurach in co-operation with
adidas-Salomon AG and the town of
Herzogenaurach
Client adviser and coordination
competitions: (phase one). Berlin,
Hans-Peter Achatzi, Benjamin Hossbach
Urban architects: A/G/P/S
Architecture, Zürich/Los Angeles, Marc
Angélil, Sarah Graham, Räto Pfenninger,
Manuel Scholl
Competition team: Marc Angélil, Sarah
Graham, Räto Pfenninger, Manuel
Scholl, Anna Klingmann, Thomas

Hildebrand, Mark Burkhard with Marco
Ganz (sculptures) and Mathis Füssler
(graphic design).
Designers of the comb-like building:
Babler and Lodde, Herzogenaurach
Designers of the staff restaurant:
Kauffmann, Theilig and Partner, Stuttgart
Landscape designers of the master plan:
Vetsch Nipkow Partner, Zürich, Gnüchtel
and Triebswetter, Kassel
Landscape designers of the staff
restaurant and comb building: Gnüchtel
and Triebswetter, Kassel
Development design: H. P. Gauff
Engineering GmbH & Co. Nuremberg
Noise control: W. Sorge, Ingenieurbüro
für Bauphysik, GmbH Nuremberg
Residual waste/waste disposal: GeoCon
GmbH, Kirchehrenbach

Pages 12–14
HSV Stadion
Type of building: stadium
Use: football stadium
Location: Hamburg, Germany
Completion: 2001
Architects: MOS Architekten (phase 1)
Studio Andreas Heller (phase 2)
Structural design: Ingenieurbüro
Günter Timm
Roof structure: Schlaich, Bergermann
and Partner
Design of outside area/landscape:
Warburg & Zwirner
Photographers: Studio Andres Heller,
Peter Stürzebecher

Page 23
Berlin-Charlottenburg Sports Hall
Type of building: large gymnasium and
sports hall
Use: double sports hall
Location: Berlin, Germany
Completion: 1990
Architects: Inken and Hinrich Baller
Structural design: Ingenieurgruppe
Berlin igb
Research, development of the rhombus
lamellae structure: Peter Stürzebecher,
Kenji Tsuchiya, Claus Scheer, Manfred
Wunderlich
Photographers: Janos Merkel, Eric-Jan
Ouwerkerk

Pages 140, 228, 229, 234, 235
Velodrome
Type of building: sports hall
Use: cycling sports hall
Location: Berlin, Germany
Completion: 1997
Architect: Dominique Perrault
Structural design: Ove Arup and
Partner
Design of outside area/landscape:
Landschaft Planen und Bauen
Photographers: Werner Butmacher,
Eric-Jan Ouwerkerk

Pages 140, 232, 233
Max-Schmeling-Halle
Type of building: sports hall
Use: multi-purpose sports hall for
martial arts and ball sports
Location: Berlin, Germany

Completion: 1997
Architects: Albert Dietz, Anett-Maud
Joppien, Jörg Juppien
Structural design: BGS Berlin
Design of outside area/landscape:
Landschaft Planen und Bauen, Rose
Fisch, Rivkah Fisch; Freiraum, Kidrich,
Lutz Neuschäfer, Barbara Willecke
Photographer: Gerhard Zwickert

Pages 140, 228, 234
Swimming Centre
Type of building: swimming pool
Use: competition swimming centre
Location: Berlin, Germany
Completion: 1999
Architects: Dominique Perrault with Rolf
Reichert
Structural design: Ove Arup, Paul
Nuttall, Allan Tweedy, Michael Schmidt,

David Deighton
Design of outside area/landscape:
Landschaft Planen und Bauen, Eric
Jacobsen
Photographers: Gerhard Zwickert,
Christian Gahl, Georges Fessy

Page 236
Vals Thermal Baths
Type of building: indoor baths
Use: thermal baths
Location: Vals, Switzerland
Completion: 1996
Architect: Peter Zumthor
Structural design: Jörg Buchli
Photographs: the Peter Zumthor archives

Page 244
Bathing Resort at Zug
Type of building: swimming pool
Use: open-air pool
Location: Zug, Switzerland
Completion:
Architect: Alfred Krähenbühl
Structural design: Ernst Moos AG
Design of outside area/landscape:
Tadashi Kawamata
Photographer: Alfred Krähenbühl

Short Biographies

Authors

Peter Stürzebecher

born in 1941
lives and works as an architect,
professor of architecture and writer in
Hamburg, Berlin and Vatilieu (Grenoble)

1962 – 1969 he studied architecture at
the Technische Universität Berlin, then
completed his industrial practical
training in Karlstad, Sweden
1978 he did his PhD thesis at the TU
Berlin on 'Das Berliner Warenhaus', Verlag Archibook, and wrote an article for
Berlin und seine Bauten, Ernst & Sohn
1969 – 1973 first architecture practice,
project leader at Werner Düttmann,
Berlin
1973 – 1981 assistant at the Hochschule
der Künste, Berlin
1976 founded an architecture office in
Berlin
1983 in Munich, in Hamburg since 1990

Professorship/visiting professorship
since 1983:
1983 – 1990 Fachhochschule Rosenheim
– interior design, scenography,
1990 – 1991 Paris École Boulle – École
Supérieure des arts appliqués aux
industries – Conceptions architecturales,
1990 – 1993 Bauhaus Dessau, Akademie
– headship of the first year,
professor of architecture at the
Fachhochschule Hamburg since 1990,
the Ecole d'Architecture de Nantes since
1997

Publications on architecture
since 1978:
1978 Worked on the Holzbauatlas 1

1978 *Das Berliner Warenhaus*,
Archibook
1978 article in *Berlin und seine
Bauten*, Ernst & Sohn
1979 – 1993 research publications of the
Entwicklungsgesellschaft Holzbau (set of
houses/'Häuserhaus',
skeleton constructions, sound barriers,
rhombus lamellae constructions)
1985 *Grüne Häuser*, Archibook
1986 Das Berliner 'Wohnregal',
S.T.E.R.N Berlin,
1988 *Szenische Architektur heute –
Stage Design*, D.A.M. Frankfurt
1989 *Berlin Denkmal Denkmodell –
EBA 2007 Nord-Express London-Berlin-
Moscow and Wolkenbügel*,
Ernst & Sohn
1990 *Paris Architecture et Utopie –
Wolkenbügel for Paris Bercy-Tolbiac*, Ernst
& Sohn
1991 *Mag Mec – das mechanische
Warenhaus*
1991 *Ein Stadttor für Berlin – Olympisches
Ensemble Paris-Berlin-Moscow and
Wolkenbügel*, Edition Aedes
1991 'Freischwinger Wolkenbügel'
Lufthansa Berlin Potsdamer Platz
and NRW, ETH Zürich Institut gta in:
Der Traum vom Wolkenbügel
1998 fashion show 'Perfekter Schnitt'
2000 *Tony Garnier/Albert Constantin*,
Edition Aedes

Exhibitions since 1980:
1980 and 1985 Berlin, Galerie Aedes,
1985 Bundesgartenschau Berlin,
1986 Zürich, Museum für Gestaltung,
1987 Rotterdam, Goethe Institut,

**Show-Dix-Platform, Hamburg, 1998.
Peter Stürzebecher, Jonas Stürzebecher,
Matthias Barschitz**

1987 Berlin Museum,
1987 Internationale Bauausstellung
Berlin
1988 Berlin, Kunsthalle,
1989 and 1990 Paris, Pavillon Arsenal,
1989 D.A.M. Frankfurt – Deutsches
Architektur Museum,
1990 Ulm, Hochschule für Gestaltung,
1991 and 1993 Bauhaus Dessau,
Akademie,
1991 Zürich, ETH, Institut gta,
1991 Montreal, Museum of Fine Arts
1992 Graz, Haus der Architekten,
1993 'Impulse' Studentenarbeiten am
Bauhaus Dessau and
1993 Experimenteller Wohnungsbau für

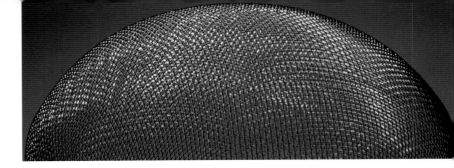

Dessau-Nord (EXPO 2000-Projekt),
Dessau/Berlin
1997 Binnenhafen Hamburg/Harburg, FH
Hamburg
1997 and 2000 Hamburg, Architektur
Sommer
2000 Berlin, Galerie Aedes

Prizes and awards:
1989 Berliner Architektur Preis –
nomination for the Wohnregal
1991 VGD Arts Prize 'the 100 best
posters of 1991' for Mag Mec
1995 Holzbau-Preis for the T-Haus
1996 Holzbau-Preis for the Columbia
swimming pool
1997 BDA-Preis des Bundes Deutscher
Architekten for the T-Haus
1997 IOC/IAKS Award for Exemplary
Sports and Leisure Facilities – awarded by
IOC International Olympic Committee for
the Columbia swimming pool
1999 AWA International Award Winning
Architecture (T-Haus)

Isestraße 76
D – 20149 Hamburg
Tel/Fax: +49 (0) 40 – 46 07 10 00
ulrichxstuerzebecher@compuserve.com

Sigrid Ulrich

born in 1954
lives and works as an economics journalist and writer in Hamburg, Berlin and
Vatilieu (Grenoble)

1974 – 1979 studied for a diploma in
economics at Ludwig-Maximilians-
Universität in Münich
1979 – 1981 German journalism school,
Münich

Employment history:
1980 – 1982 *Die Abendzeitung*, Münich
1982 – 1985 editor journalist for SWF3
radio, Südwestfunk Baden-Baden
1985 – 1987 economic correspondent for
the dpa (Deutsche Presse-Agentur, or
German press agency) in Münich
1987 – 1993 editor journalist for Manager
Magazin, Hamburg
1993 – 1999 contributor to *Die Woche*,
Hamburg
and to DeutschlandRadio Berlin since
1997
contributor to NDR radio, Norddeutscher
Rundfunk, Hamburg since 1998

Topics dealt with since 1997:
Balancing of federal budgets – the
strong against the weak
When Goliath was brought to his knees
– regional stock exchanges
National lottery – ass which rains gold
coins without inspectors
Eat or be eaten– if the audit courts
refuse amalgamation?
The reorganisation of the pension scheme
Subsidies
Who is going to wake up the sleeping
giant?
– politics and savings banks
The world is becoming increasingly
safer, yet fear is growing – a cultural
history of risk
Who are the people? 10 years of economic
and monetary union
Greed – how a new insatiability
expands
Liberalisation of the water market
Yo-yo effect: a 10 year-old slim state

Specialist events and presentations:
ARD (Arbeitsgemeinschaft der
Rundfunkanstalten Deutschlands, or the
Association of German broadcasting
corporations) Presse-Club,
Berlin – symposium on the financial
service
Hannover – symposium on the future of
banks

Isestraße 76
D – 20149 Hamburg
Tel/Fax: +49 (0) 40 – 46 07 10 00
ulrichxstuerzebecher@compuserve.com

Specialist Contributions, Reports

Niccolò Baldassini

born in 1963
lives and works in his native town of
Florence, and in Paris

-he studied architecture, aircraft and
spacecraft construction
-his final piece of work was on structural
science: 'Peter Rice, an engineer
between architecture and engineering
science'
-Masters in space technology in England
theoretical and experimental research
for the Formula 1 team from Tyrrel

Employment history and projects
(a selection):
-he works in practice and in theory as an
architect, journalist and
aviation engineer
-he is a critic for the most important
architectural magazines in Europe
Special fields (also in teaching):
engineering science and high-tech
architecture
-research into ship building and
technical design in the Renzo Piano
Building Workshop
-co-operation with the engineer's office,
RFR, Paris

RFR
4 rue d'Enghien
F – 75010 Paris
niccolo.baldassini2@libertysurf.fr

Thomas Beyer

born in 1953
he studied sport, history and educational
theory at the Universität Hamburg
leader of the Hamburger Hochschulsports
(about 25 000 participants annually, ca.
100 different types of sport) since 1979
co-author of the feasibility study for constructing a new sports building in the
Rothenbaum sports park of the
Universität Hamburg
-chairman of the 'Vereins Aktive Freizeit
e. V.' ('the active leisure time club') with
the club's own swimming pool, studio,
active nursery school and sports halls

member of the initiative circle Hamburger Forum Spielräume e. V. (supporter of numerous projects to reclaim urban mobile areas), of the 'Bewegten Schule' ('mobile school'), and also worked on involvement processes, international specialist activity in organised sport

Lectures given at the Fachhochschule Hamburg on the topic: sport in social work and Universität Hamburg, with the special area being the application of sports science for the planning of sports buildings

Hochschulsport Hamburg
Mollerstraße 10
D – 20148 Hamburg

Tel. +49 (0) 40 – 428 38 72 00
Fax +49 (0) 40 – 428 38 56 61
beyer@sport.uni-hamburg.de

Stéphane Courarie Delage

born in 1961
lives and works in Paris and Mougins
Architecte dplg

she studied architecture in Marseille Luminy from 1981 to 1984 and in Paris from 1985 to 1987
1988 diploma of École d'Architecture de Paris La Seine

Architecte Libéral since 1996
Rédacteur art-architecture at PARPAINGS (art, architecture, countryside) since 1999
editor at *TECHNIKART* (art, culture, society) from 1997 to 1999

1988 Cagnes sur mer: competition of ideas for the town centre
Project partner of Jean-François Laurent
1991 Paris: Lycée technique Diderot, Prizewinner of the International Urban Development/Architecture competition EUROPANDOM 2000
1992 Neuenstadt (D): FORCE SIGHT International exhibition of contemporary art, 31 artists, documentary video of the exhibition
1992 Warsaw: international competition of ideas, theme: restoration of the centre of Warsaw
1993 Lorient: EUROPAN 3 European competition of ideas, theme: Chez soi en ville, urbaniser les quartiers d'habitat
1993 Neuenstadt (D): BRIGHT LIGHT international exhibition of contemporary art, 29 artists, documentary video of the exhibition
1996 London: Docklands-EUROPAN 4, European competition of ideas, theme: Construire la ville sur la ville
1998 Stuttgart: conversion of the Brigitte March gallery
1999 Stuttgart: competition, Galerie der Stadt Stuttgart, with Dominique Neidlinger and Fabienne Comessie
2000 Le Vauclin (Martinique) theme: Construire la ville outre-mer, mode d'habiter et habitat, tropical

17 Boulevard Saint-Marcel
F – 75013 Paris
Tel/Fax +33 (0) 145 35 14 13

Udo Dietrich

born in 1957 in Rudolfstadt/Thuringia
lives and works as a painter and scientist in Hamburg

he studied physics and taught himself how to paint
1989 he moved to Cologne
1990 Bundesverband Bildender Künstler, Cologne in Hamburg since 1999
1995 professorship at the Fachhochschule Hamburg, specialist field: architecture

Individual exhibitions:
1993/94 ACC Gallery, Weimar
1995 TATA '95 Cologne
1996 Kölner Bank, Cologne
Altarpiece in the Church of the Resurrection, Protestant parish of Köln-Sürth, since 1995
1999 Kulturhaus Eppendorf, Hamburg
2000 Rathauspassage Hamburg
Group exhibitions:
1985 – 1999 Weimar, Nuremberg, Hürth, Berlin, Cologne, Bergneustadt, Liverpool, Cologne, Hamburg, Bremen

Semperstraße 60
D – 22303 Hamburg
Tel. : + 49 (0) 40 – 27 80 55 86

Benjamin Hossbach

born in 1966
studied architecture in Berlin
lives and works as an architect in Berlin, Partnership with Hans-Peter Achatzi in [phase one] discussions over projects concerning urban development and architecture, among others, for adidas-Salomon AG, BMW AG, and ETH Zürich.

1990 – 1995 National Contact Germany of the European Architecture Students Assembly 1994 Schinkelpreis
1995 Exhibition, 'Ölands Södra Udde' in Albrunna/Sweden
1996 – 1998 Online editor journalist of *Bauwelt*
Building Practice

Wielandstraße 40
D – 10623 Berlin
Tel +49 (0) 30 – 31 59 31-0
Fax +49 (0) 30 – 31 21 00 0
hossbach@phase1.de

Tadashi Kawamata

born in 1953 in Hokkaido

1982 Venice Biennale: Japan-Pavilion
1987 Documenta 8, Kassel; 19th São Paulo International Biennal Exhibition
1992 Documenta 9, Kassel
1996 Work in Progress, Zug until 1999
1997 Working Progress: Boat Travelling, Alkmaar (1996–1998), sculpture, Projects in Münster;
Relocation, Serpentine Gallery and Annely Juda Fine Art, London
1998 Les Chaises de Traverse Synagogue, Delme and Hôtel, Saint-Liver, Metz;
Haus der Kunst Staatsgalerie moderner

Kunst, Münich;
Every Day, 11th Biennale of Sydney;
Coal Mine Tagawa, Tagawa;
Tokyo Project: New Housing Plan
1999 Work in Progress: Project in
Toyota City, Toyota Municipal, Museum
of Art

Contact:
Kunsthaus Zug
Dorfstraße 27
CH – 6301 Zug
Tel.: 0041 – 41 – 725 33 44
Fax: 0041 – 41 – 725 33 45

Heinz W. Krewinkel

born in 1927 in Düsseldorf, died in 2000

studied architecture at the Technische
Hochschule/Universität Stuttgart

1949 – 1956 worked as an architect and
chief employee in industry; his specialist
area is design
1984–1994 editor-in-chief of *glasforum*
Co-founder and editor-in-chief of *GLAS
Architektur und Technik*
1995 – 2000 specialist leader of the
GlasKon – annual specialist convention
on glass at the trade fair in Münich

Gerokweg 8/1
D – 71032 Böblingen
Tel. +49 (0) 7031 – 23 45 52
Fax +49 (0) 7031 – 22 78 76

Sven Liebrecht

born in 1970 in Hamburg

studied architecture, maths,
music, philosophy
crafts in Guanauato, Mexico, Berlin,
Göttingen, Hamburg
received a diploma in architecture from
the Fachhochschule Hamburg

Bahrenfelder Straße 82
D – 22765 Hamburg
Tel.:+49 (0) 40 – 39 90 61 79

Frei Otto

born in 1925 in Siegmar, Saxony
lives and works in Warmbronn/Leonberg

studied architecture at the TU Berlin
1953 PhD: Das hängende Dach
1952 Opening of an office in Berlin

Employment history
(a selection):
1955 Bundesgartenschau Kassel
1957 Bundesgartenschau Cologne
1957 Interbau Berlin
1962 Deubau Gitterschale
1963 Internationale Gartenschau
Hamburg
1967 Deutscher Pavillon Weltausstellung
Montreal (with Rolf Gudbrod)
1968 Wandelbares Dach Stiftsruine
Hersfeld
1972 XX. Olympische Sommerspiele
München (with Günter Behnisch and Partner)
1974 Hotel und Konferenzzentrum
Mekka (with Rolf Gudbrod)
1975 Ceremony Tent Aberdeen (with Ted
Happold)
1975 Multihalle Bundesgartenschau
Mannheim (with Carlfried Mutschler)
1980 Münich – Volière Hellabrunn
1981 Sporthalle Jeddah (with Rolf
Gudbrod)
1982 - 1989 Holzfachschule Hooke Park
Dorset (with Richard Burton)
1987 Erweiterungspavillons Möbelfabrik
Wilkhahn (with Holger Gestering)
1990 Ökohäuser Internationale Bauausstellung Berlin (with Hermann Kendel)
1996 Pavillons Biennale Venedig (with
Bodo Rasch)
2000 Weltausstellung Hanover
Pavillons Japan (for Shigeru Ban) and

Venezuela (for Fruto Vivas)
2001 Fußgängerbrücken Mechtenberg
(with Franz-Josef Hilbers)
Research and teaching:
1958 he founded the development site
for lightweight construction, Berlin
1964 construction and running of the
Institut für leichte Flächentragwerke,
Technische Universität Stuttgart
1965 – 1990 professor at the Technische
Hochschule/Universität Stuttgart

Prizes and awards:
1970 member of the Akademie der
Künste Berlin
1980 Aga Khan Award (with Rolf Gutbrod)
1980 Doctor of Science h.c., University
of Bath
1982 Honorary Fellow RIBA Royal
Institute of British Architects London
1982 first prize from the BDA, Bund
Deutscher Architekten, and gold medal
1986 Honorary Fellow Institution of
Structural Engineers, London
1989 International Design Award, Japan
Design Foundation
1990 Honorary Doctor at the University
of Essen
1990 Honda prize for environmental
technology, Honda Foundation
1992 Werkbundpreis Bayern
1996 first prize from the Deutscher
Architekten- und Ingenieurverband
1997 Wolf Prize in Arts, Jerusalem
1998 Aga Khan Award for Architecture
(with Nabil Fanous, Ted Happold)
1998 Premio Especial VII Bienal de
Architectura de Buenos Aires
2000 medal for merit, Baden-Württemberg,

2000 honorary patent of citizenship from the town of Leonberg

Exhibitions:
1971 'The Work of Frei Otto', MOMA Museum of Modern Art, New York
1975 'The Work of Frei Otto' revised version, international travelling exhibition over five continents
1981 'Natürliche Konstruktionen', Institute for Foreign Relations, Stuttgart and in Goethe Institutes in approximately 80 countries
1992 'Gestalt finden, Frei Otto – Bodo Rasch', exhibition entry for the Werkbundpreis, Villa Stuck, Munich

Publications:
1954 *Das hängende Dach*, Reprint 1990
1962/1966 *Zugbeanpruchte Konstruktionen*, Band I und II
1982 *Natürliche Konstruktionen*
1984 *Frei Otto – Schriften und Reden* 1951 – 1983
1988 Gestaltwerdung
1969 – 1998 39 publications for the Institute for Light Surface Structures
Atelier Frei Otto Warmbronn
Berghalde 19
D – 71229 Leonberg
Tel +49 (0)7152 – 410 84
Fax +49 (0) 7152 – 439 08

Ulrich Pramann

born in 1950 in Sieber/the Harz mountains
lives in Wörthsee/Upper Bavaria

Deutsche Journalistenschule, Munich

has written texts, reports and books on sport, health, fitness and careers since 1975
editor of *Stern* magazine
reporter for *Welt am Sonntag*, presenter on Deutsches Sport Fernsehen
editor-in-chief and editor of *Fit for Fun*

Publications – more than 20 books, among which are the bestsellers:
Einfach wohlfühlen, 6th edn
Perfektes Lauftraining, with Herbert Steffny, 13th edn
Kleine Philosophie der Passionen – Laufen Fit für den Marathon
So haben Sie Erfolg, with Jörg Löhr, 4th edn
Mehr Energie fürs Leben, with Dr. Spitzbart, Jörg Löhr, 3rd edn
Einfach mehr vom Leben, with Jörg Löhr, Erfolgstrainer
So schützen Sie Ihre Gesundheit, with Dr. Müller-Wohlfahrt, 6th edn
Ich fühle mich so richtig gut, with Katarina Witt – 2001
Lauf dich schlank! – 2001

Am Steinberg 7
82237 Wörthsee
Tel +49 (0) 8153 – 86 08
Fax +49 (0) 8153 – 86 11

Ulrich Stock

born 1959
lives and works in Hamburg

reporter for *Zeit* in Hamburg
Stock@zeit.de

Martin Wimmer

born in1928 in Weimar
lives and works in Berlin

studied architecture in Weimar and Dresden, his dissertation was called: Der Einfluss der Olympischen Idee auf Städtebau und Architektur (The influence of the Olympic ideal on city building and architecture)

1956 – 1990 Deutsche Bauakademie in Berlin, Institute for Urban Development and Architecture he taught at the Technische Universität Dresden and at the Humboldt-Universität Berlin, on sports and leisure buildings among others
He worked in international organisations on plans including for the Olympic Games, the 'Olympische Spiele Berlin 2000'

Publications:
Olympischer Alltag – Bauten für Sport und Freizeit in der Welt von Morgen

Rosenfelder Ring 121
10315 Berlin
Tel.: +49 (0) 30 – 529 16 30

Architects and
Structural Designers and Engineers

Note: specialist contributors are denoted by (S) after page number

Index of Photographers for the Specialist Contributions

The photographers whose images were used in the international projects
are listed in the project catalogue

**'Sports Campus Saint Nazaire',
Gaël Marec and Sebastian Morel
German-French Seminar 1999,
Fachhochschule Hamburg and
Ecole d'Architecture de Nantes
Peter Stürzebecher, Jacques Dulieu**